# CAMBRIDGE LIBRARY COLLECTION

*Books of enduring scholarly value*

## History

The books reissued in this series include accounts of historical events and movements by eye-witnesses and contemporaries, as well as landmark studies that assembled significant source materials or developed new historiographical methods. The series includes work in social, political and military history on a wide range of periods and regions, giving modern scholars ready access to influential publications of the past.

## Christ, St Francis and To-day

Medieval historian G.C. Coulton relinquished his own holy orders in 1885 but remained firmly engaged with Christianity. This 1919 collection of lectures is a radical and impassioned discussion of how Christianity must change to meet the needs of post-war society as soldiers return from the trenches. Drawing parallels between the lives of Jesus Christ and St Francis of Assisi, Coulton highlights how ambiguities in the surviving accounts of both men have diverted the original course of their ministry and, with it, the objectives and outlook of the church. The author also takes on the weaknesses in both Catholic and agnostic arguments and advocates a simplifying and democratisation of Christianity and the resolving of denominational differences. Included alongside the lectures is the author's comprehensive response to a number of questions raised by the original lecture series which provides a useful conclusion to the controversial anti-Catholic's plea for religious modernisation.

T0370952

Cambridge University Press has long been a pioneer in the reissuing of out-of-print titles from its own backlist, producing digital reprints of books that are still sought after by scholars and students but could not be reprinted economically using traditional technology. The Cambridge Library Collection extends this activity to a wider range of books which are still of importance to researchers and professionals, either for the source material they contain, or as landmarks in the history of their academic discipline.

Drawing from the world-renowned collections in the Cambridge University Library, and guided by the advice of experts in each subject area, Cambridge University Press is using state-of-the-art scanning machines in its own Printing House to capture the content of each book selected for inclusion. The files are processed to give a consistently clear, crisp image, and the books finished to the high quality standard for which the Press is recognised around the world. The latest print-on-demand technology ensures that the books will remain available indefinitely, and that orders for single or multiple copies can quickly be supplied.

The Cambridge Library Collection will bring back to life books of enduring scholarly value (including out-of-copyright works originally issued by other publishers) across a wide range of disciplines in the humanities and social sciences and in science and technology.

# Christ, St Francis
# and To-day

G.G. COULTON

CAMBRIDGE UNIVERSITY PRESS

Cambridge, New York, Melbourne, Madrid, Cape Town, Singapore,
São Paolo, Delhi, Dubai, Tokyo, Mexico City

Published in the United States of America by Cambridge University Press, New York

www.cambridge.org
Information on this title: www.cambridge.org/9781108010399

© in this compilation Cambridge University Press 2010

This edition first published 1919
This digitally printed version 2010

ISBN 978-1-108-01039-9 Paperback

# CHRIST, ST FRANCIS
# AND TO-DAY

CAMBRIDGE UNIVERSITY PRESS

C. F. CLAY, Manager

LONDON : FETTER LANE, E.C. 4

NEW YORK : G. P. PUTNAM'S SONS

BOMBAY ⎱
CALCUTTA ⎰ MACMILLAN AND CO., LTD.
MADRAS ⎰

TORONTO : J. M. DENT AND SONS, Ltd.

TOKYO : MARUZEN-KABUSHIKI-KAISHA

# CHRIST, ST FRANCIS
# AND TO-DAY

BY

## G. G. COULTON, M.A.

OF ST CATHARINE'S COLLEGE

CAMBRIDGE

AT THE UNIVERSITY PRESS

1919

The author's special thanks are due to the Editor of *The Hibbert Journal*, who has permitted him to reprint in Chapter II the greater part of an article which appeared in that *Journal* last October.

TO THE BEST OF MY SCHOOLMASTERS

E. G. H.

WITH ABIDING GRATITUDE AND RESPECT

In quanto sine peccato possumus, vitare proximorum scandalum debemus. Si autem de veritate scandalum sumitur, utilius permittitur nasci scandalum quam veritas relinquatur.

S. Gregorii Magni Homiliarum in Ezechielem<br>lib. I. Hom. VII. § 5.

Le plus grand dérèglement de l'esprit, c'est de croire les choses parce qu'on veut qu'elles soient, et non parce qu'on a vu qu'elles sont en effet.

Bossuet, De la connaissance de Dieu et de soi-même, Chap. I. § 16.

Wrap not yourself round in the associations of years past; nor determine that to be truth which you wish to be so, nor make an idol of cherished anticipations. Time is short, eternity is long.

J. H. Newman, An Essay on the Development of Christian Doctrine, 1845, ch. xii.

# PREFACE

THESE lectures were delivered to a mixed audience at Cambridge during the Michaelmas Term of 1918, and I must heartily thank those hearers and friends whose criticisms have enabled me to explain or correct the text. If the notes and appendix have thus swollen to many times the bulk originally contemplated, it may still be hoped that some readers will find, here and there, more than a controversial interest in this supplementary matter.

G. G. C.

GREAT SHELFORD
*January*, 1919

# CHRIST, ST FRANCIS
# AND TO-DAY

## I

DURING my last two years of study among the early
Franciscan records with history pupils, we have been
frequently confronted with problems too exclusively religious to come within the scope of the Historical Tripos.
Therefore I have been tempted more and more to seek a
wider audience before whom these questions might be discussed, free from the necessary restrictions of the Tripos, and
in equal freedom from the conventions of the pulpit. Now,
or never, is the time to test our ultimate beliefs. On what
do they rest? How far are we prepared to modify them, if
necessary? And how far *is* such modification necessary, if
we are not to be left clinging to unrealities in a real world;
if we are not to sacrifice what is and what shall be to the
shadow of that which might possibly have been instead, if
God had willed the education of the human race to be other
than it actually is and has been?

It seems increasingly probable that one of the most fatal
intellectual limitations of the middle ages was due to the
divorce of religious and philosophical and political discussion from ordinary private life—a divorce not complete,
of course, but still very serious. In those days, men lived
in one language—if I may so put it—and philosophized in
another; they lived in the mother tongue, and tried to
think their higher thoughts in Latin. Therefore the
specialist had little chance of appealing to the man in the
street; and—more fatal still—the thoughts of the man in
the street were not a constant atmosphere which the

specialist was compelled to breathe whether he would or would not. This metaphor of *atmosphere* may, I think, be pressed very literally and very far: the more we believe in democracy, the more we shall be inclined to recognize that the thoughts of the multitude, and the little practical difficulties of daily life, form a broad, out-of-door breezy air which blows an infinity of cobwebs away. Nor is its work negative only; for it is also an atmosphere laden with the germs of many ideas destined to fertilize specialist and abstract thought, whenever the crowd and the specialist can come into frank and natural contact. We get this contact in ancient Greece, and we get it in the modern world. But I think it was scarcely possible for any man in the middle ages, however favourably situated, to sit over the fire with one or two intimates and discuss freely the most intricate problems of life, in a language not only capable in itself of expressing the finer shades of thought, but also fully available in this particular case. For, though the Latin language may have supplied, in the abstract, all that was required, yet very seldom indeed was that language possessed, both by the speaker and by the listener, in such perfection as to elicit those finer and more delicate tones without which there can be no full interchange of ideas on the deepest subjects. Once at least, even in the middle ages, this barrier was to some extent broken down; and we have there one of the most interesting chapters in the history of medieval thought. At the close of the thirteenth century, the Dominicans found serious difficulties, as other orders found at different times, with their dependent nunneries. At one time they cut the knot by leaving the nuns entirely to themselves. But this proved unworkable; and the final decision was that the nunneries should regularly be supplied with teaching friars, but that these teachers should be chosen only among the *docti fratres*— the senior university lecturers. These maturer scholars, deputed to teach the nuns had a whole language to create;

it was necessary not only to find vernacular terms for the concepts of scholastic philosophy but also to simplify those concepts themselves so as to bring them within the comprehension of women whose education was of the most rudimentary sort. The *docti fratres* had to translate the language of the intellect into the language of the heart. But here we have precisely Goethe's definition of mysticism; 'the scholastic of the heart.' Therefore, in those districts of the Upper Rhine where not only the Dominicans were more thickly planted than anywhere else in Europe, but nunneries also were disproportionately numerous even among the Dominicans, there grew up that school of mystic theology, preponderantly Dominican, which gradually became one of the elements in the Reformation of the sixteenth century. The *docti fratres* constantly shaped their thoughts for the women, and were constantly stimulated themselves by the ideas which the women gave them in return; for this counter-influence is a matter of recorded history. You will find it noted, for instance, in the autobiography of the great mystic Suso. Under this cross-fertilization, therefore, it was natural enough that a school of thought should grow up not only fresher and more natural than the formal teaching of the universities, but destined also to advance far in directions in which the universities, left to themselves, seemed least willing to go forward.

To these mystics we may probably trace, however indirectly, such English mystics as Juliana of Norwich, at whose cell-window many came to listen whose thirst after God was not fully satisfied by the official church. From Juliana and such as she derived Margery Backster the carpenter's wife of Martham in the same county, who taught 'that it was more religious to eat [on Fridays] the fragments [of meat] left on Thursday at night, than to go to the market to bring themselves in debt to buy fish[1].' It is possible that all the professorial lectures of the later middle ages did less to prepare for the Reformation than these Dominican lectures to nuns. Thought and life were here fused together by a flame of passionate desire for truth; and there is something of that same passionate desire in many quarters at the present moment. The real world—the after-war world —calls upon us to neglect those limitations which are often implied in the epithet *academic*, and to take another step forward in the democratization of thought.

It has become a commonplace to remark that this war will sweep away many stale conventions; and that we have entered for ever into a new world of freer speculation and franker speech. But a commonplace has its dangers: cynics might argue that this extraordinary unanimity is painfully suggestive of lip-homage, and that, if *war-work* is the universal catch-word for the present, and *reconstruction* for the future, these words often cover a lurking hope that others will do the work while we shall have done the talking. In actual fact, are not most of us here present situated like that young officer whose first fight Mérimée describes with such extraordinary vividness? While the shells and bullets fell round him, he felt a solemn elation at the thought that he stood in the midst of one of the great battles of the world, yet unharmed and serene. We, too, go on repeating to ourselves that this world-war is one of the greatest and most terrible phenomena of all recorded history; yet many of us all this while—those to whom fate has been most lenient, or who are naturally least sensitive to outward impressions—many of us, I say, and perhaps I might truly say, most of us, must confess with some sense of shame that this life of 1918 bears, under the surface, a painful resemblance to the life of 1913. We say to ourselves that this is the last fight of unabashed autocracy against democracy, and the first fight of a rudimentary world-league against traditional world-anarchy: but in which army are we serving, if only with the service of those who stand and wait? Meanwhile, all those who are most entitled to be heard are warning us with one voice that the real stress, for the country in general, will come when the war is over. How and where it will arrive, is not always so easy to predict; but, beyond all doubt, there is coming upon us a real fire which will burn up much of the chaff and stubble of civilization; a real revolution which will make short work of a thousand unrealities. There cannot have been many periods of history in which the writing has stood out so clearly upon the wall, and yet time has been so liberally allowed to prepare for the crisis, as now. Few generations can have stood so nearly as we do in the position which the Jewish people occupied when the Baptist began his preaching: 'Repent ye, for the kingdom of heaven is at hand.' To them, as to us, the impending crisis was vague; but it was fraught with infinite possibilities of good and evil; and its menace called imperiously upon every soul to face the future, before the truth should burst like a flood upon the world. Moreover we need not yet forecast in detail all that is presently to come upon us, in order to see clearly enough the main things that it behoves us already to do. Directly peace comes, millions of men will return from the trenches; and it is these men who will count. They will bring the spirit of the trenches with them—a spirit of loyal comradeship as against hard outward facts and bitter personal enemies—a spirit of actual present comradeship with each other, and of potential future comradeship even with the enemy. They will bring, we are told, a deeper sense of religion than before, even though it be no more than a broken and incoherent cry for the kingdom of heaven, intermingled with much that must prove strangely disconcerting to official theology. In that spirit they will come; and in that spirit we must be ready to meet them, with all that we can muster of the soldier's loyal comradeship, the soldier's courage in the face of danger and suffering, and that belief of the soldier in his righteous cause which justifies, and even necessitates, implacable hostility towards the enemy so long as that enemy is still formidable.

It seems worth while to dwell briefly on each of these three points in turn.

(1) Comradeship in thought is surely the first and most essential of the three. We must do all that we can to find common ground, from which, even though all further advance may be in divergent directions, yet each at least can see all along the other's line of progress, because he follows it systematically from the general and agreed starting-place. Thus, and thus alone, can we avoid those gratuitous confusions and misunderstandings which are the most fruitful causes of separation. There is a very great deal common even to the two extremes of catholic and agnostic; and, in religious as in secular life, everything depends on our finding this common ground. We hope that, after the war, capitalism may be found far more ready to look upon wealth as a trust rather than as a possession by divine right; and that labour, on the other hand, may be more ready to accept the capitalist's concessions as at least an interim solution, until times are ripe for further advance. So also there seems good cause for hope that, in this hard school, the men who come back to us will have found a possible concordat in religion; that the one extreme will be found more ready to acknowledge man's inextinguishable yearning for something more than pure reason can supply, while the other extreme has realized that faith, if it reaches out beyond reason, must still be purged of all that is contrary to reason.

But must we not say that in religion, as in economics, it is doubly incumbent upon the richer party to meet the other more than half way? Lazarus at the gate of Dives is not so pitiable as the average man at the porch of a church which counts for nothing to him[2]. And, if the war has not advanced us in other ways, at least it has helped us a little to realize the duty of those who have towards

those who have not. It has at least worked us all up to
a certain moral heat; the stuff of the human mind has
become more malleable. Those who have Christ have a
more human Christ than before; those who have him not
begin to conceive humanity with an emotion which is
already *naturaliter Christiana*. Christian and secularist are
ripe for agreement on the old terms rehearsed by the author
of *Piers Plowman* 500 years ago:

'...Jesu Christ of heaven
In a poor man's apparel pursueth us ever...
For on Calvary, of Christ's blood, Christendom gan spring,
And blood-brethren we became there...and gentlemen
each one[3].'

Before the war, religious reformers were visibly haunted
by the blank indifference with which they had to contend
among the general public. The world was not so much
hostile to them as dead; a valley of dry bones...'Son
of man, can these bones live?' (Ezekiel xxxvii. 3)....
There was far more of passive than of active resignation
in the churchman's answer: 'O Lord God, thou knowest!'
To-day our mood is rather the active resignation of that
brief dialogue which Carlyle loved to quote: 'Then said
his Lordship, "Well, God mend all!"—"Nay, by God,
Donald, we must help him to mend it."' And this feeling
that the old state of things simply *cannot* continue is, if not
sentimentally hottest, at least most reasonable and therefore positively strongest in those who, having most to lose,
have also most to give. The prudent capitalist is already
calculating how far he can raise wages without involving
capital and labour in one common failure. And many men
of splendid ecclesiastical traditions—many religious capi-
talists, as we may phrase it—are asking themselves equally
narrowly: 'How far can I safely treat these traditions of
mine as non-essential, for the sake of an understanding, if
not an actual union, between traditionalist and anti-

traditionalist? Did God indeed mean all men to be saved
and to come to a knowledge of the truth? If so, grave as
must be the responsibility of the multitude which will not
hear me, still more grievous is my own fault when I suffer
any merely human tradition, however hallowed in its
associations, to stand between the outsider already soft-
ened towards religion, and the Christ to whom I have so
long called him in vain.' Jesus loved the rich young man
who had kept all the commandments from his youth up;
but one thing fatally separated that young man from a
real understanding of the poor; that is, of the vast
majority of mankind. Is that truth valid only in economics, and not in religion? Is not the churchman often
impotent before the unbeliever just because he is choked
with his spiritual riches, and has not even an elementary
comprehension of the unbeliever's real state of mind? He
has inherited a comfortable faith as others inherit a comfortable income; neither he nor they realize what sweat and
tears it cost, or even what blood, to accumulate originally
that stock of faith or money. If the sense of comradeship
cannot remedy this, if the churchman will not now make
all possible concessions voluntarily for the sake of his
blood-brethren of Calvary, he will soon have to make them
under the pressure of sheer necessity[4].

(2) For (and this brings me to the second point) we are
confronted now with bitter facts which were scarcely
better able to command attention five years ago than the
fact of the German menace. Everybody realizes now what
only a few ventured to preach then. If, some six years
ago, one of the most distinguished theologians of this
university insisted that we no longer live in a Christian
world, this austere gospel is preached now by a great cloud
of witnesses from the battle-front[5]. There is no question
to-day of unsettling minds by repeating what nobody seems
to contradict; the only question is, how to reconstruct these
masses of past tradition which, by common consent, lie

already in confusion; and, again, how to buttress up much more that seems tottering to its fall. Orthodoxy is fast losing both its numerical superiority and its prescriptive possession of all debatable territory. The believer is already compelled to sit down and consult whether he be able, with ten thousand, to meet the unbeliever that cometh against him with twenty thousand. The thoughtful agnostic, on the other hand, is now brought to ask himself seriously whether his own reverence for reason, and the general claim of supreme authority for reason, be not tainted with the idolatry of the market-place; whether he be not an agnostic because his friends are agnostic. In the face of present facts, both sides are brought more nearly to something like the conclusion expressed a century ago by William Blake: 'man must and will have some religion[6].'

(3) Thirdly, we all see more clearly than of old that, though things and persons can be separated in logic, and though we must always remember the real distinction here, yet we are constantly compelled to take them together in practice. Fine distinctions between the harm that an individual German may do, and the innocence of Germany in general, are seen now in their true perspective. We note that the men who urge such distinctions most vehemently are those who, even before 1914, were not always in touch with concrete realities; and that this original bias has been vastly exaggerated by the shock of the war. Perhaps there never will be an age in which the public will be more ready to acknowledge that God's war against the evil *thing* implies also a commission to war inexorably against the evil *man*, so long as he not only does evil but believes in evil, and hopes for victory in and through evil; that, so long as he is a power for evil, he must be dealt with as an evil thing, and only when we have disarmed him can we take him to mercy and bind up his wounds. That reminder is as necessary in the field of religious enquiry as it is on the

field of battle. It is not only that, under the easy-going mood of our long peace, we had drifted too much into the habit of condoning many half-forgotten crimes in the past with something of that detached and contemptuous indifference with which Tennyson's Northern Farmer made allowances for the sermons under which he sat week by week. '*The weight of opinion is against me*' (said Lord Acton in his inaugural lecture here at Cambridge, marking thereby his protest against the general indifference):—'The weight of opinion is against me, when I exhort you never to debase the moral currency or to lower the standard of rectitude, but to try others by the final maxim that governs your own lives, and to suffer no man and no cause to escape the undying penalty which history has the power to inflict upon wrong[7].' But there is more than this. There is, I believe, no department of human thought in which easily accessible facts, and the explicit evidence of unimpeachable documents, have been, and still are, so flagrantly violated as in religious discussion; and this not only where philosophical subtleties are concerned, but even on what should be the plainer ground of church history. Editors of so-called religious papers refuse to insert corrections of verifiable facts quite as obdurately as the editors of the most frankly partisan journals in worldly politics. In higher quarters, things are still worse. A cardinal of the Roman church in England has reprinted deliberately, in the interests of his own party, misstatements of fact so gross, and so easily verifiable, that he might just as reasonably have printed a denial of the spelling of his own name[8]. He has done this not because the matters were so small as to escape his notice, but for the very opposite reason; because they were so essential to his theories that to confess the plain truth, under correction, would have been to confess shame and defeat. It was far easier to go on under the safe assumption that scarcely one reader in a hundred has leisure or opportunity to verify

historical references, and that the plain facts of his falsi-
fication, as I have stated them here, must seem quite incredible to all who have not thus verified; in other words,
that 99 per cent. of his readers will still retain, for some
time at any rate, some sort of belief in his accuracy, whereas a frank and open retractation would have shaken his
credit among his own party. We are sometimes told that
things are just as bad at the other end of the religious pole.
If that be so indeed—and it has yet to be proved—then
here is one more explanation of the now admitted fact
that our soldiers, in coming back from the trenches with
more real religion, will return with even less tolerance for
official religion. We have long been reaping the fruits of
what Dr Rashdall stigmatized, years ago, as the appalling
indifference of religious disputants to easily verifiable
facts. We shall always have the theologians we deserve,
and the religious historians we deserve; if, therefore, we
are ever to stand in religion upon the firm ground of the
serious soldier, we must assure ourselves first of all that
no man and no cause shall escape the undying penalty
which history has the power to inflict upon these wilful perversions of plain fact. This will not interfere with our
sincere repetition of the Lord's prayer, if only we lay equal
stress on all the clauses, first judging ourselves, that we be
not judged. Among the deepest causes of religious differences have always been mutual distrust, and the suspicion
of unfairness on both sides. If this is to be remedied, the
children of light must now imitate, however tardily, the
business honesty of the children of this world; and a man's
printed word must become as trustworthy as his signature
to a cheque[9].

If these words seem too strong—yet I doubt whether
milder phrases will seem possible to anyone who troubles
to verify the facts—still, in any case, let me hasten to add
that the laxer judgments of which Lord Acton complained,
and the general indifference to those yet more indefensible

perversions of which he was not directly cognizant, are in a great measure due to generosity, and a generosity not always mistaken. If we are to err at all, by all means let us err on that side, at least in dealing with persons. In painful consciousness of our own blunders, let us make the widest reasonable allowance for original motives of error, as apart from unrepentant persistence in errors once plainly exploded. But for the erroneous statement itself, or the erroneous idea, there is no room for mercy in real historical study. Lord Acton's protest was probably called out by Creighton's *History of the Popes*, in which Creighton's generosity found excuses where Acton could find none; and in which—it may be said with due deference—there is a general tendency to grant points good-humouredly to what the author considered the weaker party, Roman catholicism. But we have no moral right to grant points in history; they are not ours to grant; the thing is as unjustifiable as playing ducks and drakes with public money. We are trustees for other readers and thinkers, present and future; nor can we calculate the final consequences of the smallest distortion of the truth, however generous in its original motive. Was there ever a legend more amiable or more respectable than those which represent all the early Christian martyrs as having met their fate with serene joy, and which speak of the odour of sanctity that emanated from their corpses or their bones? There, if anywhere, scepticism might go good-humouredly on its way and leave the edifying illusions undisturbed. Yet it was precisely these legends which evidently went a long way towards reconciling an able, pious and kind-hearted Christian to such systematic cruelties against his fellow-Christians as would have revolted his mere natural sense. The Blessed James of the Mark, one of the most Franciscan of the sons of St Francis, wrote a pamphlet about 1450 A.D. against the *Fraticelli*, the Franciscans who had been driven into revolt by the unfranciscan and intolerant conduct of their

brethren and of the official church. He convinces himself
that they are heretics, and deserve the persecution they get,
by the following reasons among others. First all catholic
doctors count it as a property of the true faith to grow
under oppression and tribulation, as appears in the days
of the martyrs, when a hundredfold more were converted
than killed; but, on the contrary, this new sect has
dwindled under our attack, in spite of certain powerful
protectors whom it had at first. Secondly, God works
wonderful miracles through St Bernardino of Siena on our
side, who has been officially proved and recorded to have
raised twenty-three dead folk to life; 'but in you' (pursues
the pamphleteer, addressing the Fraticelli) 'God works no
miracles, except that in burning ye stink as rotten flesh....
For example, certain heretics were burnt at Fabriano when
pope Nicholas was there, and the stench went through the
city for three whole days; which I know myself, because it
came for those three days even unto the convent wherein
I dwelt[10].' If only this good man could have realized that
the savour of a burnt Christian under Nero had been even
as the savour of a burnt heretic, and that thousands of
early Christians had escaped death by denying their faith,
he would have been readier to listen to reasonable protests
from the heretics of his own day. And we may find a fairly
close parallel to this in our own days. Newspaper correspondents, for at least the first year or two of the war,
thought it necessary to celebrate constantly the supposed
'joy of battle'; even the early numbers of *The Daily News*
would probably be found liberally peppered with this or
equivalent phrases. It has been easy, under cover of this
pious falsehood, for us to persuade ourselves that we may
leave the 'joy of battle' to our soldiers, and take for ourselves the joy of 'business as usual,' by a fair exchange in
which is no robbery. Meanwhile, however, truth filters
slowly in, and there is some hope that this lie, at least,
may be not only dead before the men come back, but put

well out of sight as a thing that corrupts the air. Yet, when this is gone, there are many others behind it to be cleared away.

Our first task, then, is largely a negative task. The wreckage of many traditions is now generally admitted; and it is our business to cut away all wreckage, whether secular or religious. We want to get things fairly clear before the men come home. We want them to see that we have taken some pains to make sure that the dead shall not have died in vain, and that the living shall not henceforth live in vain. Then the soldier, for his part, will help us to see what vital force there is in freedom from convention, and in a comradeship that sinks all minor differences in face of tremendous odds. Moreover, there is a negative side even to this idea of comradeship; for we can attain to it only by renunciation—or at least by temporary renunciation—of much that is dear to us as individuals. Catholic and agnostic cannot stand for a moment on common ground unless each will first concede a great deal; not finally indeed, by any sudden abandonment, but at least tentatively and hypothetically, as Euclid sometimes asks us to do for the sake of clearing our minds. Or, if that is asking too much, let each at least try to put himself in imagination in the other camp, and let us ask ourselves what outlook is possible from that point of view. We shall then see, perhaps, that this gulf which too often divides thinking people from each other cannot possibly be so hopeless, under any circumstances, as the gulf which divides all thinking people from those who will not or dare not think. However deeply one side, or both sides, be entangled in error, yet the cause of sincere catholic and agnostic as against thoughtless error is a common cause.

Here, again, let me go further and deeper for a moment, since it would be affectation to ignore not only the possibility that both extremes of religious thought may be represented in this audience, but also the practical

certainty that we do represent almost every shade between those extremes.

On the one hand, what does the agnostic lose by
recognizing the strength of the catholic case? The existence of Christianity, to begin with, is the most remarkable
fact in all recorded history. The belief in a crucified
carpenter has taken more men out of themselves, and
taken them further out of themselves, than any other
belief of which we have cognizance. Roman catholics, if
we take account of their numbers and discipline together,
form the most conspicuous of Christian bodies. They have
a theory to justify their present constitution and creed
which is on the whole remarkably coherent, and which, if
it is to be disproved, cannot easily be disproved except by
the removal of certain historical supports to which the
agnostic has seldom given real attention. Nor has the
agnostic, as a rule, formed even an ostensibly sufficient
theory to account for the nineteen hundred years of
Christianity. If, as the philosopher in *Sartor Resartus*
suggested, religion be really a secretion of the lower intestine, then science could undertake few greater tasks
than the location and analysis of that secretion. If it be,
as Gibbon thought, a sort of epidemic plague, let us set
ourselves here again to isolate and neutralize the bacillus.
Or finally, if the scientific student has no inclination for
these things, let him at least recognize that this is not his
glory, but one of his limitations. Few people who have
really studied the history of Christianity—few, even,
among those who have studied it closely as it exists among
us at present—would be prepared to dismiss it as a phenomenon unworthy of scientific enquiry. It would seem
not too much, therefore, to ask of the agnostic that he
should say in his own mind of the catholic: 'Here is a
specialist in a real department of study. He has, what
I have in my own department, faith; that is, he forms
hypotheses which he tries to test (I speak of course of the

true and fearless catholic) in the light of observed facts. However I may disagree with him, I have no right to quarrel with his faith: on the contrary, we must all be grateful to all others who honestly try to work out a hypothesis, whatever it be. His facts I must and will check wherever I can; but, even so, we are fellow-labourers in the same field; and truth will be justified of all her children.'

To the catholic, on the other hand, may we not plead that he should study his own history, and admit the besetting dangers of a great and imposing past? Must we not say that, as it is the agnostic's duty always to face seriously the possibility of the catholic's being right, so it is the catholic's duty to admit the contrary possibility? Must he not face the fact that it was precisely the noble past of Judaism—its great religious traditions and the devoted loyalty with which it kept its inheritance as a sacred and inalienable trust—that formed one of the greatest obstacles to the spread of Christianity? The heir is almost certain to lack that just sense of values which is natural to those who first amassed the inheritance; he is tempted to cling to trifles as essential, and to lock up the essential in a cupboard or even cast it away. 'Christians are not born, but made'; so wrote Tertullian, one of the earliest and greatest of the Christian fathers; and St Jerome said the same two centuries later[11]. No man is born a Christian; and, except on the most mechanical theory of the sacraments, he who is not conscious how he found the faith must in honesty ask himself whether he has really got it yet.

If, then, we are all to set out truth-seeking together in the after-war spirit, can we ask less of the two extremists than that each in imagination should put himself so far in the other's place? and, when we ask only this much, can either reasonably refuse?

But again I ask your leave to speak more freely for all

the rest of these lectures, as to an audience of actual or potential believers, who feel that nothing Christian can be quite devoid of interest to fellow-Christians. *Christianus sum, Christiani nil a me alienum puto*; if we had of real Christianity only so much as a grain of mustard-seed, there would perhaps be no after-war problem.

Yet here, on the very threshold of the subject, an objector might stop us to ask: What is a Christian? Different answers have been given at different times and in different places, but I hope to make it credible, as we go on, that the earliest and most orthodox definition would have been as simple and comprehensive as that only definition which can satisfy the awakened sense of reality in these latest days—a Christian is a man who is, in his degree, a follower of Christ, just as a Gladstonian or a Darwinian is a follower of Gladstone or of Darwin[4]. In all such cases there are infinite possible degrees; in all such, again, one man will deny another man's right to the name; but, just as every real follower of Gladstone was really a Gladstonian, whatever any club or caucus might decide to the contrary, so to be a Christian it is only necessary to try, however imperfectly, to follow Christ; and the church of Christ is the multitude of those who are thus trying after their own fashion. This is the common-sense definition, and this seems to me the plain definition of gospel history; for even a good many conservative critics are willing to admit the possibility of interpolation for those two passages of St Matthew's gospel which speak of the church in the spirit of a later time (xvi. 18 and xviii. 17). Few things are more striking, in all these nineteen centuries of Christian records, than the unwillingness of churchmen to adopt this broadest definition, and their difficulty in agreeing upon any other. If membership of the church of Christ was not clearly and officially defined by its Founder from the very first, this was certainly not for lack of opportunity, since the question arose in a sufficiently acute form even

while he was with us (Luke ix. 49 and x. 25: Mark iii. 22).
We read how John, the beloved disciple, said to him 'Master, we saw one casting out devils in thy name, and we
forbad him, because he followeth not with us. And Jesus
said unto him: Forbid him not; for he that is not against
us is for us.' To the lawyer, again, who asked: 'What shall
I do to inherit eternal life?' the answer was not that he
must first join some visible body of disciples, but that he
should model himself on a man of another religious de-
nomination—the Good Samaritan. These, by themselves,
would seem to constitute the plainest and broadest charter
of toleration; but we are reminded that Christ, on another
occasion, seems to have spoken differently: 'He that is not
with me is against me, and he that gathereth not with me
scattereth abroad' (Matt. xii. 30). It is strange that those
who see here a contradiction of the earlier charter of liberty
should pay so little heed to the context of both cases. In
the first, a man was doing the work of Christ and his
disciples, but after his own fashion; he went with them in
the spirit, though in the flesh 'he followeth not after us.'
For him the Lord decrees not prohibition, but sympathy.
In the second case the Pharisees, men who were not themselves doing Christ's work, presumed, on the strength of
their official position and from behind the ramparts of their
traditional religion, to condemn even the good that Christ
did because it was not done in the good way, in the only
orthodox way. That it *seems* good, they cannot deny, but
to admit that it *is* good would be to abandon their whole
exclusive position, and to proceed with shame to take the
lowest place. Therefore this apparent good must be glossed
as concealed evil; Christ's seeming virtue is a diabolical
illusion: 'This fellow doth not cast out devils but by
Beelzebub the prince of the devils.' In this case, says the
Lord, he that is not for us is against us. He who cannot
bow before plain goodness when he sees it, and who cannot
even give it the ordinary grudging recognition 'of course

this isn't as good as *our* goodness, because this man is not
one of us; but still it's wonderful what the fellow is con-
triving to do in his own bungling and unorthodox fashion'
—he whose traditions and whose inherited privileges tempt
him to mistake the finger of God for the devil's finger—
that man is poisoned at the very core of his heart, and
poisons all that he touches. This is the one unforgivable
sin (Christ went on to say): this is the sin against the Holy
Ghost. Unforgivable, in the sense that it inexorably brings
its own damnation with it. The man who sees evil in good
itself cannot logically stop short of worshipping the devil,
since the devil is the only power we can trust never to
shock our feelings by any disconcerting display of uncon-
ventional goodness.

But this is anticipatory, though a necessary anticipation; it will be my task in a succeeding lecture to touch
very briefly upon the earliest and the latest theories of
church membership. I will only say meanwhile that I have
never met any definition of the visible church (including
of course the *teaching* church, without which a mere
definition of membership is of little practical use), which
is at once clear in its provisions for inclusion or exclusion,
and reconcilable with historical facts. It is remarkable
how unwilling the greatest men have been to commit themselves here. It is easy to find definitions so vague that
historical criticism can lay no hold on them; or, again, to
find clear-cut definitions which rest upon blindness to
historical facts. I can make no claim, however, to exhaustive study here; and if anyone in my audience can
refer me to a definition both clear and accurate, I shall be
very grateful. Meanwhile I ask you to accept this as a
working definition: that *the Christian is one who tries, in
some degree, to follow Christ*; or, if not to accept it, at least
to bear in mind that this is the sense in which I always use
the word. As things stand at present, our best hope of a
lasting settlement is to go to the root of the matter at

once. The only consideration which justifies the further waste of a single human life on the Western front is the conviction that a patched-up peace could mean not the end of war but its perpetuation. In the conflict of ideas, also, there are periods when it is no real counsel of peace that we should refrain from wounding opposing beliefs, so long as no wound is wantonly or maliciously inflicted. Destructive and constructive work may be completely separated in logic, but very seldom in practice. Who is more creative than a great sculptor like Michael Angelo, of whom it was said that he saw with his bodily eyes the yet unshaped statue, and that his chisel seemed only to be stripping off the outer husk which hid the inner reality? To him, every blow meant not the destruction of a costly block of marble, but the liberation of a living soul from its shroud of circumstance; and of him it is recorded by his fellow-artist Cellini that, at eighty, he would knock off more marble in an hour than a younger man of twice his bodily vigour. The iconoclast of the present is often far truer than the traditionalist to all the best inheritance of the past; the destruction of a wilderness of ivy is a reconstruction of the original building that it hid.

The illusions of the extreme conservatives, both in politics and in religion, spring from a false historical perspective. These men are not so much inspired, as hypnotized, by the great names of the past; they are crushed, and would fain crush us, by the reflection that those were greater men than any in modern times. But, so far as this is true, let us never forget how those great men showed their greatness in nothing so much as this, that they helped to make possible our own better world of to-day; *our own* not in the sense that we made it, but simply that we have inherited it. Those men sowed good seed, not always knowing what would spring from it; and it would be no due respect for them, but rather untruth to their memory, if we for our part failed to reap where they have so loyally

sown, and then to go forward ourselves, ploughing and
sowing for the future. If we fail in this duty, we shall reap
the reward not of those who ventured forth their talents
and received them again with usury, but of him who laid
up reverently in a napkin that which had been given him
for the wear-and-tear of daily use. Every honest reformer
may justly encourage himself with that song in which
William Blake looked both backward to Christ and forward
to Christ from amid the hell of the industrial system in his
day, reading into the future all that had been most divine
in the past:

> 'And did those feet in ancient time
>     Walk upon England's mountains green?
> And was the holy Lamb of God
>     On England's pleasant pastures seen?
>
> And did the countenance divine
>     Shine forth upon our clouded hills?
> And was Jerusalem builded here
>     Among these dark Satanic mills?
>
> Bring me my bow of burning gold,
>     Bring me my arrows of desire,
> Bring me my spear—O clouds, unfold,
>     Bring me my chariot of fire!
>
> I will not cease from mental fight
>     Nor shall my sword sleep in my hand
> Till we have built Jerusalem
>     In England's green and pleasant land[12].'

Let us repeat it, all who thus strive to clear the way for
the future are more loyal to the divine tradition than those
who brood upon the past in barren immobility. All that
was greatest in former ages was striving to anticipate this
world that we live in; nor is there any greatness in our own
present except so far as we also are striving to evolve a
better world for our children. That is the spirit in which

we must meet our returning soldiers—the conviction that all the materials of the new Jerusalem lie scattered already everywhere at our feet, if we would but bend down and stretch out to seize them. Socialism is moving heaven and earth to make ready for this coming opportunity; if our own religion be as living as socialism is, we for our part shall neglect no precaution to that end, and shrink from no sacrifice

# II

SINCE these lectures originated in detached historico-theological difficulties which presented themselves in a particular field of study, you will not complain, I hope, if they are rather disjointed in detail. But in one way they aim at complete continuity, as keeping certain principles constantly in sight. One of these was stated in my first lecture, where I urged the necessity of religious views which should answer to the quickened sense of reality, and the robuster tone of mind, produced by this war. I tried to show that this necessary reconstruction would be impossible without a certain amount of destruction; that the building of Jerusalem among these dark Satanic mills involves active mental warfare; that we cannot be true to all that was best in the past without hating and trying to destroy all that is worst in the present world. And I pleaded that we should begin by making as clean a sweep as possible, each in his own mind, of all temptations to treat as indisputable those things which separate us from many other thoughtful people, while they leave us still associated with multitudes of the thoughtless. The conviction, for instance, that Christ's words to St Peter definitely promised supremacy over the whole church not only to him personally but to all who claim to be his successors, separates the extreme catholic from whole sections of the thinking world, but not from unthinking thousands within his own communion. On the other hand, if an agnostic bases himself upon the *a priori* impossibility of miracles, he again, on this one point, is at variance with hundreds of thinking folk, but in unison with thousands of the thoughtless; for nothing is easier than to disbelieve without serious enquiry. But, while this reflection should convince each man individually of the duty of never closing the door

entirely against any possible reconsideration of these
points—while (further still) such serious differences among
thinking men may legitimately suggest that questions
which are still so undecided after 1900 years can scarcely
be so essential to man's well-being as other matters upon
which civilized humanity is now pretty well agreed—yet,
in urging both these points, we are not for a moment asking
either of the rivals actually to surrender his own considered
belief for the sake of pleasing other people, or even for the
far greater gain of merging religious differences in religious
co-operation. We are only asking each to put himself
hypothetically, and to begin with, on common ground with
the other. I do not see how anyone who refuses this concession can complain if he and his friends find themselves
gradually left high and dry in a progressive world. It is
fatal to stand altogether apart from the multitude, unless
indeed it be at one of those most exceptional moments
where the minority has in it such a consuming fire of truth
as will not only kindle the sacrifice but lick up the very
water in the trench. At the top of p. 14 of the Report of
the Archbishops' Second Committee of Inquiry as to the
state of things revealed by this war, there stand eight
melancholy words which do the greatest honour to the
spirit in which the English church is facing the facts now:
'It is their hearts which we have lost.' *We*, in this sentence,
are the clergy: *their hearts* are the hearts of the poor. Let
us meet frankness with frankness, and admit how unfair
it would be to take this single sentence too exclusively or
too literally. Again, even if it were exclusively and literally
true, let us admit how unfair it would be not to saddle the
flock with its full share in this estrangement. But it does
roughly express a fact which must be treated as fundamental by all who are seriously struggling for a better world
through religion—by all who weigh their own words when
they pray daily 'Thy kingdom come.' Those eight words
mean at least this, that the church can no longer go on

saying to the multitude 'If only you would put yourselves first upon my ground, I could show you God's will.' The man in the trenches now says with brutal plainness what millions had drifted into thinking inarticulately: 'If you have God's word in your mouths, come over here to us. We will listen greedily to any ideal that bases itself upon the hard common-sense regulating our daily lives. If only you will start with us on that ground, we will go along with you to all higher things that you can show us.' For (though the ecclesiastical eye is often tempted to overlook this), even the hardest common-sense has in it not only the germs, but also far more than the bare germs of comradeship, of self-sacrifice, of actual present love for wife and child and friend, and potential love for God and all fellow men. If the church has faith as a grain of mustard-seed, she will no longer rely mainly upon her chiding message of the past—a message which would create future difficulties even if it were accompanied, as it is not at present, with the efficacious act:—'Hear now, ye rebels, must we fetch you water out of this rock?' (Numbers xx. 10).

This, then, is the text of the present lecture; that the church will never regain her hold on the masses, until she makes herself a great act of faith. It was the Chartists, I think, who first christened the pulpit 'cowards' castle.' To capture the modern trade unionist, you must meet him on his own ground. For the war's sake, the trade unionist has himself made this sacrifice. He has put off, provisionally and hypothetically, much of the armour in which he had trusted to defend himself against capitalist exploitation. We are preaching to him now that he will find it beneficial to society, and for his own good also, to abandon those things not provisionally, but for ever. Let us do more than preach; let us show him the way. Let the Christian be known by this: that he 'lays aside every weight, and runs with patience the race that is set before

him, looking unto Jesus, the author and finisher of our
faith' (Heb. xii. 1).

Here then, let us suppose, is the church daring at last
to step down upon neutral and common ground in her own
sphere of religion, even as the workman has dared for our
sake to accept neutral ground in economics. The church,
let us say, will do what she can, tentatively and hypothetically, to waive those claims which have gone so far to
lose her the hearts of the poor. What then, we must ask,
is the weight which most impedes her race at present?
and, what, therefore, should first be cast aside? Some may
answer, *sacerdotalism*; but this can hardly be; if you
followed the reports of the recent Wesleyan Congress in
the daily papers, you will have noted that the language
there was as frankly pessimistic as in the Archbishops'
report. I am afraid we must go deeper still. What most
separates the churchman inside from the man in the street
outside, is the current ecclesiastical conception of physical
miracles. The multitude is slipping away from the
Wesleyan, as from the Anglican and from the Catholic.
You may test this for yourselves; in every serious religious
discussion, the argument will soon settle down to this
question of miracles. In our discussions of Franciscan
history it was, I think, the first question raised by the
pupils in the first conversation class; and if, on succeeding
occasions, it cropped up less frequently, this was only because it was felt to be a question too definitely theological
for exhaustive treatment in an history class. From that
time forward, I was resolved to take an early opportunity
of discussing it before a wider audience.

In the official life of St Francis by Thomas of Celano,
written at the pope's bidding within two years of the
saint's death, and within a few months of his canonization,
we find this remarkable sentence: 'Those corporeal
miracles sometimes *show* sanctity, but *make* it not.'
These are unexpected words, you will say, from a most

orthodox writer of the thirteenth century; and Thomas must have had some strong reason for them. His reason seems fairly obvious when we reflect for a moment. Miracles were cheap in those days, and Celano knew that, in marvels of the vulgar kind, his hero would ill compete with other saints who had not been worthy to loose the latchet of St Francis's shoe. Moreover, Celano knew that many men still doubted the reality even of St Francis's stigmata; and he must have known, even if he himself had not shared, the involuntary mental reservations of some who had known St Francis in the flesh. On this point we have the most valuable evidence from Celano's friend and fellow-missionary Jordan of Giano, whose autobiography is one of the frankest and most trustworthy of early Franciscan records. Jordan tells us, in his fifty-ninth chapter, how he once received an unusual and enthusiastic ovation attributable only to his own personal popularity or to the occult virtues of some hairs of St Francis and fragments of the saintly frock, which he bore secretly upon his person. As a modest man, he disclaimed for himself, and gave all the glory to the relics, adding: 'From that time forward, brother Jordan began to hold the blessed Francis in greater reverence—for he had seen him and known him in this present life as an infirm man, and therefore something of human weakness had clung to him— thenceforward, I say, he held him in greater reverence and honour, seeing how God inflamed the hearts of the brethren by the Holy Ghost and would not suffer the relics of his [holy person] to remain unknown.' To Jordan, this *corporale miraculum* brought a deeper reverence for St Francis; but Celano, in the face of similar, if less marked, hesitations, seems consciously to throw his main weight upon the far safer ground of St Francis's spiritual miracles. In this, it need hardly be added, he is imitated by modern Roman catholic biographers of irreproachable orthodoxy, such as Father Cuthbert and Mr Jörgensen.

But it is still more important to note that Thomas's apologetic words are not his own, and that they form part of a far franker pronouncement on this subject by one of the greatest popes of the middle ages—by the pope who converted England. Gregory the Great is, in a sense, the pope of the miraculous. His *Dialogues*, one of the most popular books of the whole middle ages, may almost be said to have given an official stamp to the then rudimentary doctrine of purgatory. The book is one long string of marvels, some so vulgar and trivial that it is difficult to understand how this great man could have taken them so seriously. Yet Gregory had his definite reasons for this emphasis on the miraculous. Like other medieval chroniclers of visions, he tells us that these stories which he alleges are brought together in order to confirm the fainting faith of his age[13]. He was an honest man who honestly believed in these things not only as facts, but as facts that would tend to Christian edification. However, as an honest man accustomed to 'dress and undress his soul' in solitary meditation, Gregory in another place frankly faces the fact that God's kingdom cometh not with observation, and that those of whom Christ complains 'except ye see signs and wonders, ye will not believe' are to be stigmatized as Jews or Judaizers. Moreover, he was not afraid plainly to proclaim this. We have a homily of his 'preached before the people of Rome, in St Peter's basilica, on the feast of our Lord's Ascension\*.' He took for his text Mark xvi. 14 ff. and his very first words struck the keynote of the higher faith. 'That our Lord's disciples were slow to believe in his resurrection, was not so much through their infirmity (if I may so speak) as for the confirmation of our own faith. For, whereas they doubted of the resurrection, it hath been shown unto us by many proofs; which when we read and acknowledge, what else is this but a strengthening of us through their dubitations? for I am less

---

\* Bk II. no. 29.

comforted by Mary Magdalene, who was swift to believe,
than by Thomas, who doubted so long. He, in his uncertainty, touched the very scars of his Lord's wounds: and
thus hath he removed the wound of doubt from our
breast.' Then, when he comes to vv. 17-18, 'These signs
shall follow them that believe: in my name shall they cast
out devils, etc.,' St Gregory continues: 'Now, my brethren,
seeing that ye work no such signs, is it that ye believe
not? Consider that such signs were necessary in the beginnings of the church. For, in order that the multitude
of them that believed should grow unto faith, they needed
to be nourished by miracles; for we too, in planting young
trees, water them busily until we see that they have at
last taken firm hold of the earth; then, when their root is
once firmly fixed, we water no more. Hence it is that
St Paul writeth [1 Cor. xiv. 22]: "Tongues are for a sign,
not to believers but to unbelievers."'

'Moreover, we have matter for still subtler consideration
with regard to these signs and wonders. For indeed holy
church worketh daily now, in the spirit, whatsoever the
apostles then wrought in the body. When her priests, by
the grace of exorcism, lay hands on a believer and forbid
that any evil spirit dwell in that man's mind, what is this
but to cast out devils? And when the faithful, leaving the
worldly speech of their former life, attune their lips to
sacred mysteries and proclaim to the utmost of their
power the praise and might of their creator, what is this
but to speak with new tongues? Moreover, in removing
malice from other men's hearts by their pious exhortations,
do they not take up serpents? When, again, they hear
pestilent persuasions yet are unmoved to evil deeds, do
they not then drink a deadly poison, yet take no harm?
And whensoever, seeing their neighbours to grow faint in
good works, and hastening to succour them with all their
might, they confirm by the example of their own good
deeds these stumbling brethren—do they not then lay

their hands upon the sick, that they may be whole? And indeed these miracles are all the greater for being spiritual; all the greater, in as much as they lift up not the bodies but the souls of men. Such signs as these, beloved brethren, ye yourselves work by God's help, if ye will. Now, those other outward signs avail not to gain life for the men who work them; for such bodily miracles sometimes show us to be holy, yet do not make us holy—*nam corporalia illa miracula ostendunt aliquando sanctitatem, non autem faciunt.* On the other hand these spiritual miracles, wrought in the mind, do not show but make the power of life. The former are possible even to wicked men; the latter cannot be enjoyed but by the righteous. There are some of whom he said, who was the Truth: "Many will say unto me in that day 'Lord, Lord, have we not prophesied in thy name, and in thy name have cast out devils, and in thy name done many wonderful works?' And then will I profess unto them, 'I never knew you; depart from me, ye that work iniquity!'" Wherefore, my beloved brethren, love not those signs which ye may share in common with the reprobate; but love such as I have already said, miracles of charity and piety, which are the more secure as they are the more secret, and whose reward from God is by so much the greater as their glory among men is less.' Here, then, is a train of thought very difficult to reconcile with that other side of medieval Christianity which not only survived the Reformation but may be said, perhaps, to be still dominant in the official church. It would seem impossible to make St Gregory's words mean anything less than this, that physical miracles alone cannot prove the truth of a religion; while, on the other hand, moral miracles can do so, even apart from any question of the physical miracle. From which it would follow that the question of physical miracles is, at best, a secondary question to the student of Christian evidences. And this position is strengthened, as will be seen presently, by the fact that those who have

most insisted on physical miracles have also been most
ready to grant that the devil, as well as God, can work
such miracles—or at least, can seem to do so, which comes
to the same thing for evidential purposes. Startling as it
may seem, this train of thought is not altogether new; for
Origen had foreshadowed it in his controversy with Celsus.
He found himself compelled, like all his contemporaries,
to admit the existence of Pagan as well as of Christian
miracles; and therefore he fell back to some extent
on the immeasurably greater moral significance of the
latter[14].

A considerable portion of St Gregory's homily is read
once a year in the services of the Roman church, but none
of the words above quoted are thus immortalized. Yet
they found their direct echo throughout the middle ages;
and others, who possibly had never read St Gregory, came
to the same conclusion as he.

Ekkehard Minimus, dean of the great monastery of
St Gall (about 1090 A.D.) wrote the life of his fellow monk,
Notker Labeo, author of that funeral anthem: *In the midst
of life we are in death.* To excuse himself for having no
miracles to relate, he expressly refers to St Gregory's
words, then five centuries old. Again, the writer of a remarkable contemporary life of St Bernard of Tiron (who
founded a new congregation of Benedictines and died in
1117) falls back upon the same plea. So also does the
biographer of St Stephen of Obazine, writing about a
century later. He pleads: 'When we write a saint's life,
men specially require of us that we should record his
miracles.... To awaken sinners to eternal life is a greater
miracle than to awaken them from bodily death.' Even
more interesting are the words of Odo of Cluny, the saint
who may really be said to have founded the great Cluniac
order. He recurs repeatedly to this subject in his *Life of
St Gerard of Aurillac,* his *Sermon on the burning of St
Martin's at Tours,* and his *Collationes*\*. In the former

\* Migne, *P. L.* vol. 133, col. 65, 87, 157, 536.

books, he had to defend the two saints against the suspicion of thaumaturgic impotence. In the last, he had to deal with the prevalent belief that the world was in its last stage, and the reign of Antichrist imminent—a belief which he himself shared and which was by no means peculiar to his generation (about 940 A.D.). Odo was a diligent student of Gregory, and writes, if anything, with less reserve than his master. There is (he says) a season to everything under heaven; the church did need physical miracles in the days when a handful of fishermen and artizans were striving to convert emperors and high priests; but the faith is now settled on a firm enough foundation to dispense with them; our motto should be *The just shall live by his faith.* If miracles are ceasing in our day, this is because God wishes to search men's hearts; for 'the followers of Antichrist shall work miracles, in order that those who revere the church only for the sake of her miracles may cease to venerate her, and may transfer their allegiance to Antichrist.' 'When these Judaizers seek after signs, what do they make of John the Baptist, who is recorded to have worked no miracle since his birth?' 'Many men have worked miracles of whom the Judge will say, "I never knew you." But those who do works of piety are they to whom it shall be said, "Come, ye blessed of my Father."' So far St Odo of Cluny. All these words are the more enlightening, as coming from a man who was believed by his contemporaries to have wrought many miracles. St Odo doubtless knew that he himself had wrought no *miracula corporalia*; he must have suspected the authenticity of many other popular miracles; and being a real saint, he fell back upon the kingdom of God within his soul. Lastly (to take only one more example) we may find a somewhat half-hearted admission of what may be called the Gregorian doctrine in St Thomas Aquinas, who holds that miracles detract from the merits of a faith which will not believe except through miracles*.'

* *Summa Theologiae*, pars 3. q. 43. iii. 3 m. Cf. *Contra Gentiles*, IV. c. 55.

So far the Gregorian tradition; but there is another even more interesting line of medieval thought parallel to this, and going back (as almost everything does when we find leisure to trace it) to St Augustine. The idea in question is most tersely and pointedly stated by Dante*: 'If the world turned to Christianity without miracles, this [one miracle, in itself] is such that the others are not worth the hundredth of it.' The Augustinian passage from which this is concentrated runs as follows†: 'It is incredible that Christ should rise again in the flesh, and carry it up to Heaven with Him. It is incredible that the world should believe this, and it is incredible that this belief should be effected by a small sort of poor, simple, unlearned men. The first of these our adversaries believe not; the second they behold, and cannot tell how it be wrought, unless it be done through the third.... If they believe not that the apostles wrought any such things for confirmation of the resurrection of Christ, it is sufficient then that the whole world believed them without miracles, which is a miracle as great as any of the rest.'

Here, then, if we accept Augustine and Dante with all their logical implications, we find all *corporalia miracula* cast into the same limbo of irrelevance to which an extreme modernist would banish them to-day. If indeed it be the most wonderful miracle of all that the greatest event in recorded history—the rise and spread of Christianity—should have taken place without the aid of lesser miracles; if it be true that the spiritual miracle is actually heightened by the abandonment of physical miracles, why should we not dare this venture of faith and shake ourselves altogether free? Not, indeed, as denying the possibility of these physical miracles, which would simply be an inverted dogmatism, but as frankly recognizing their progressive irrelevance, and as refusing to be separated

* *Parad.* xxiv. 106.
† *De Civ. Dei*, Bk xxii. chap. v. last paragraph.

from our fellow-Christians by differences on this ground, just as St Paul refused to admit any separation under Christ between the circumcised and the uncircumcised.

To any mind which is willing to recognize development in religion (and development has become, since Newman, a word as orthodox in catholicism as it is in science) one glance backward will cast a flood of light on this Augustinian idea. There is no philosophical problem which may not be illustrated from even the driest facts of history; and Herder was probably right in contending that the next great stride in human civilization will be taken when men begin to take the actual deeds and thoughts of past humanity no less seriously, and to eliminate error no less impartially, than in their study of crystals or of gases. The task is certainly more difficult: but the difficulty is only a measure of its importance to civilization. Let us therefore see what historical basis we may find for these two converging lines of argument, the Gregorian and the Augustinian, as to the progressive irrelevance of *physical* miracles (to adopt the distinction made implicitly by one author and explicitly by the other). Let us go back to the days when, as Odo puts it, the kingdom of heaven was preached to an incredulous world by 'fisherfolk and lowly artificers.' Let us turn to the fountain head, to the gospels. There we read: 'When John had heard in the prison the works of Christ, he sent two of his disciples and said unto him: Art thou he that should come, or do we look for another?' Nothing could have been easier to Jesus than to answer with a plain *Yes* or *No*, thus making up their minds for them. But he preferred in fact to throw them back upon their own private judgment: 'Go and shew John again those things which ye do hear and see'—the physical and moral miracles to which their own senses might bear direct testimony. Presumably there was enough evidence here to convince every honest enquirer.

But what is that evidence to us? What was it already

to Augustine and Gregory, when we examine it strictly?
for Christ's own words prescribe a strict examination in
this matter. John's disciples had the testimony of their
own senses. John himself had the evidence of witnesses
whose personal equation he could measure to a hair's
breadth; we, on the other hand, have the evidence of a
tradition long current orally before it was committed to
writing, and admittedly retouched in places since that first
written record. Moreover, social circumstances and human
mentality have changed and changed again during these
nineteen centuries; it may almost be said that, from the
strictly scientific point of view, the cogency of this evidence
varies with the square of the distances. What man would
be so rash as to stake all his invested sayings upon written
testimony no stronger, from the historical point of view,
than this record of nineteen centuries ago? Who would
take it as sufficient that the text itself was unimpeachably
authentic, and that the facts there asserted had been
accepted without question by millions of reasonable human
beings? We should not dream of staking our money on
such evidence for a physical miracle, and if in this case
men are still willing to stake their very lives on the Ever-
lasting Yes, it is because they recognize that the whole
centre of gravity has shifted since John first asked the
question. To men who saw the lame walk and the blind
receive their sight, or who were surrounded on all sides by
fellow-citizens talking of these things, it was easier to decide that Jesus must be the Messiah; from the physical
they argued to the spiritual. To us, it is only the spiritual
belief in Jesus which makes it possible for us to think
seriously about his physical miracles. We can easily test
this. We have only to imagine the discovery of some admittedly authentic Persian manuscript recording the
physical miracles, 1900 years ago, of a man whose spiritual
preaching had been colourless and whose wider influence
had been null. Apart from philologists and folk-lorists,

nobody would even pretend an interest in them. Already
to St Augustine, fifteen centuries before us, it was mainly
the spiritual miracle of Christianity which rendered the
Christian miracles credible; and this change of balance has
become more marked with every succeeding century.

We must not, however, look upon this change of ground
with regard to miracles as conscious or constant. A few
men, as we shall see, tried to look both deep and far; but
most medieval theologians seem to have kept as much as
possible to colourless generalities or to have dealt with
occasional difficulties in detail[15]. But such difficulties were
forced again and again on thinking men by the thoughtless
materialism of the multitude; and, in default of code-law
on this question, we may gather from medieval writers
a good deal of case-law. It may be well to quote a few
concrete instances.

Matthew Paris, in his *Lives of the Abbots of St Albans*,
tells us how Abbot Leofric (about 1020 A.D.) planned to
save St Alban's bones from the Danes. The monastery of
Ely, amid its fens, seemed comparatively safe; to Ely
therefore he commended the precious shrine; but, being an
Abbot himself, he took his precautions even against the
monks of Ely. He secretly walled up the real bones at
St Albans, and commended a false set with all due pomp
to his fellow-Abbot's generosity. The Danes came and
went, and the 'treacherous' monks of Ely 'excogitated a
fraud.' They too sent back the shrine with all pomp and
ceremony: but with the substitution of 'certain adulterine
bones.' The original contents they kept themselves: 'and,'
writes Matthew Paris in righteous contempt, 'let them
keep the same, if it be their pleasure, to all eternity!'
St Albans knew where the real bones were; but unfortunately Nature did not; the unhallowed bones worked
miracles at Ely. Confronted with this problem, Matthew
Paris soars into more spiritual regions. 'If then our holy
martyr be so honoured at Ely; and if, being so honoured,

he works miracles there, then we of St Albans ought to
desire that he may be believed to have left his bones in
every great church within this realm of England. Thus
will he get the greater honour, and be worshipped in the
greater number of places.' The story is typical; it was the
materialism of the many which forced the few into im-
material regions of thought. Matthew Paris, by habit and
perhaps by preference, took the lower view of miracles.
But when this concrete case showed him that the lower
view implied the triumph of Ely fraud over St Albans
truth, then his sense of patriotism and of truth raised him
for a moment to what is practically the Gregorian standpoint[16]. Take Guibert of Nogent again, a man of real distinction in Anselm's and Abelard's generation. Guibert
was indignant that there should be one John Baptist's
head at Amiens and another at Constantinople; in one
case at least, he argues, the worship of this relic must be
idolatrous*. But Sir John Maundeville, nearly two centuries later, is already on a higher plane. He was by this
time confronted not with duplicate, but with triplicate
heads; yet, after a tentatively rationalistic explanation,
he falls back upon the philosophic conclusion: 'Nevertheless, howsoever men worship him, doubtless the blessed
John is satisfied[17].'

We have already seen Origen and St Gregory and St Odo
facing the notorious but embarrassing fact that bad men
might work real miracles: that there were miracles both of
the devil and of God. This was universally admitted: nor
is this admission affected, from the present point of view,
by such an argument as Origen's, that the devil cannot
really work these miracles, but can only make it seem to
men's senses that such have been wrought. This obviously
leaves the *corporale miraculum*, as evidential proof, just as
weak as it was before. It was puzzling then, that a miracle
might be either God's or the devil's; and even more

* *De Pignoribus Sanctorum*, lib. I. c. III. § ii.

disconcerting must have been the fact that good men were ready to work false miracles. Guibert of Nogent, by far the most honest and uncompromising opponent of the furore for relics and miracles among his contemporaries, does nevertheless justify one fraudulent miracle wrought at the first Crusade because it was successful*. Again, the good friar Salimbene of Parma tells us in the same breath of true miracles worked by his fellow-friar Gerard of Modena, and of gross frauds which this same Gerard concocted to impress the public which flocked to his mission-sermons†. These were cases which frequently came up for decision in the court of conscience, and which must always embarrass every generation which shrinks from that venture of faith to which St Augustine and St Gregory may point the way, even if they do not consistently lead us thither. But indeed Christ's own words would seem to remove every reason for separating ourselves from those who suspend their judgment as to physical miracles. If signs and wonders had been essentials, on the strength of which one Christian is morally bound to deny another Christian's claim to brotherhood, Christ could scarcely have uttered those words of rebuke: 'Except ye see signs and wonders ye will not believe.'

But some may say: 'This is but a single text; elsewhere the gospels leave us no option but to accept a great many physical miracles.' I propose to deal with this very important objection in my next lecture.

* *Gesta Dei per Francos*, lib. IV. c. XVII.
† *Mon. Germ.* XXXII. p. 76.

# III

I PROMISED in my last lecture to deal with the obvious
objection that the gospels leave us no excuse for suspension of judgment on the question of miracles. Here, the
analogy of Franciscan history throws a flood of light upon
gospel history. A whole book might be written—and ought
long ago to have been written—on this subject; but a few
brief hints must suffice for this evening. I will here try to
assume nothing as a certain fact but what is admitted by
thoughtful students on all sides—fully admitted, for instance, by Mr N. P. Williams, a Fellow of Exeter College,
who has lately printed in *The Church Times* a series of
sermons expressly directed against the modernist party in
the Church of England, and who may conveniently be
cited as an unexceptionable witness here.

The earliest existing Christian documents date from
more than twenty years after Christ's death; these are the
first of St Paul's epistles. The gospels, as Mr Williams reminds us, 'belong to the second generation*.' The first
written, St Mark's, is never dated earlier than forty years
after the crucifixion. Forty years, in the long perspective
of history, is a very brief space indeed. When an authentic
document can be shown to be 1860 years old, it seems
hypercritical to emphasize its evidential inferiority to a
similar document 1900 years old. Rough common-sense
might pronounce this difference of only 2 per cent. to be
practically negligible; and yet historical sense (which is,
after all, only patient common-sense applied to history)
sees all the difference in the world between the two. Those
to whom these forty years seem negligible are using the
wrong end of the telescope. If we carry our mental vision
back to the crucifixion, instead of looking at it all from the

* *Church Times*, April 26, 1918, p. 315, col. 3, top.

standpoint of 1918 A.D., we shall see this at once. Things
were moving rapidly in those days, as they have been
moving for the last four years in Europe. A few months
before then—not even a few years, but a few months only
—the apostles were convinced that their Master was to be
an earthly king. Then, for a moment, he seemed to be
nothing at all and dead and gone. Then, again, they saw
him glorious and immortal—a spiritual king for ever and
ever. All these changes, let us again remind ourselves,
occurred within the space of a few months. Or, again, let
us take the whole period of forty years which we are now
discussing. While the earlier portion of this period saw
Saul breathing threatenings and slaughter against everything Christian, the later period saw in him the apostle
who did more than any other to spread the knowledge of
Christ. Again, while the earlier years found the church
conscience-bound in bondage to circumcision, the later
years heard her preaching a gospel in which neither circumcision nor uncircumcision availeth anything, but a new
creature. To the historian, the question from which of
these years a particular document dates must often be
essential. We have only to think for one moment of the
changes of individual judgment, and the positive revolu-
tions in national policy, which we ourselves have witnessed
in the last four years, in order to realize that even a well-
informed writer of 1954 might, in perfect honesty, visualize
the thoughts of 1914, and even the events of 1914, after a
pattern which would render him a most untrustworthy
historical guide in detail, though his general outlook might
be wonderfully accurate. This is a common-sense reflection
to which we may choose to close our own eyes, but which
we cannot possibly hide from the man in the street. In
any world of reality no creed can survive which claims
strict historical evidence, as apart from the inward evidence of the spirit, for doctrines which history is unable,
in the very nature of the case, to guarantee. Mr Williams,

for instance, begins by pleading the very ancient and ex-
tremely probable tradition that our earliest gospel, St
Mark's, represents the substance of St Peter's verbal
teaching, which the evangelist had heard repeated for
years and years before he committed it to writing. Therefore, argues Mr Williams, this gospel 'represents what is,
for practical purposes, first-hand evidence as to our Lord's
life*.' Coming presently to the last chapter of St Mark's
gospel, he writes 'the crucial passage is short—only fourteen verses—but going back, as we know that it does, to
St Peter, and through him, therefore, to the eyewitnesses,
Mary of Magdala and Mary the mother of James, it is
enough to guarantee for all time the cardinal fact of the
empty tomb. It is not extravagant to claim that this
passage is equivalent to an affidavit made by the women
to the effect (a) that they visited the tomb of Jesus less
than forty-eight hours after his burial, and (b) that they
found the tomb open and the body gone.' These are the
words of a theologian familiar with modern textual
scholarship, who has confessed a few sentences before that
the accounts of the three synoptic gospels contain dis-
crepancies of detail which are difficult to explain. He
admits that St Peter (according to St Mark) was dependent
upon what he heard from the two women; moreover, that
we do not possess St Mark's gospel exactly as he wrote it.
Peter, therefore, heard it at secondhand from the women,
and Mark at third-hand from Peter: and Mark's gospel,
written at least forty years after the event, has certainly
undergone later changes in the course of its transmission
to us. To talk of this, then, when we cannot even be
absolutely sure that we have St Mark's words at all, as
'practically an affidavit from the two women' is to base
the orthodox creed upon a confusion of thought, and a
licence of speech, which can only repel those who are really
trying to face the facts. In no branch of the actual business

* *Church Times*, May 3, p. 333, col. 2, top.

of life does an honourable man permit himself more licence than a barrister pleading in court for his client. But what barrister would venture to risk his reputation by pleading before a British jury that what $A$ tells to $B$, what $B$ repeats over and over again to $C$, what $C$ writes down forty years after the event (probably when $B$ is dead), and what has come down to us, even so, in a document which admittedly contains subsequent modifications, is practically equivalent, as evidential proof, to an affidavit from the original $A$? The men who have seen reality will never be won by this kind of talk. It can only render them angry and contemptuous; and the Archbishops' Committee may sit down and write further: 'It is their intellects that we have lost.' For this is only part of a long cumulative process. Here, for instance, is a similar argument put forward on a far more important occasion, by a still more distinguished Oxford scholar than Mr Williams. In the *Bampton Lectures* for 1859, Mr Rawlinson, brother of the famous Oriental scholar, undertook to support the Mosaic authorship and authenticity of Genesis in the following words. 'Adam, according to the Hebrew original, was for 243 years contemporary with Methuselah, who conversed for a hundred years with Shem. Shem was for fifty years contemporary with Jacob, who probably saw Jochebed, Moses's mother. Thus Moses might by oral tradition have obtained the history of Abraham, and even of the Deluge, at third hand, and that of the Temptation and the Fall at fifth hand.... It must be allowed (even on mere human grounds) that the account which Moses gives of the Temptation and the Fall is to be depended on, if it passed through no more than four hands between him and Adam [18].' It is impossible to read this seriously now-a-days, though these words were solemnly pronounced before the university of Oxford not sixty years ago, and received with equal solemnity by large numbers of able men. The use of random language in reasoned defence of Christianity dates from so long ago, and is still so common, that it is absolutely necessary to seize every opportunity of casting the light of reality upon it. It would be most calamitous if, by a long process of natural selection, the Christian became the person who can accept such reasoning as this without qualms of conscience. Let us therefore follow Mr Williams's arguments a little further; for he is one of the most distinguished among the churchmen who travesty the gospel message by this unwarrantable confusion between moral and historical evidence; and it is on account of his distinction that it seemed worth while to quote him textually here. The very facts that he instances show us how God meant the gospels not to be taken uncritically, not to be brought down like the Ark of God in the hope that their mere presence would hustle the Philistines off the battlefield, but to be reverently scrutinized like other documents, and used with the caution which all sacred things deserve. The original ending of Mark (Mr Williams reminds us) has been lost; verses 15 to the end of the last chapter are the work of one whom he calls 'some ingenious scribe' of two generations later*. He goes on: 'By what we may reverently consider a special exercise of Divine Providence, the unknown person, 1800 years ago, who tore off the last page of St Mark's Gospel, was just restrained from tearing off the fourteen verses which show us that St Mark—and therefore his informant St Peter—believed in the empty tomb.' Here, then, all careful readers are on common ground; Divine Providence willed that the earliest Christian records, like other historical documents, should not be preserved by any physical miracle from mutilation, from interpolation, or even from total destruction: for we know that not only Pauline epistles but even sayings of our Lord have been lost. God has chosen that those which survive should live, like many other documents, by the moral miracle of their intrinsic value. It is pretty generally

* *Church Times*, May 3, p. 333, col. 3, top.

admitted that nothing ever penned by man has been so accurately transmitted over such a length of time as the New Testament, when once the Canon had been formed; but, even so, the defects of transmission have been sufficient to remind us that these books were in fact penned by man: and theologians of all schools have now abandoned, at least in theory, that faint-hearted and mistaken reverence which forbade even the sincere comparison of the canonical scriptures with other books. On all hands it is felt that we possess only a fraction of what we might have had, and that this fraction is sometimes of painfully doubtful historical certainty. It is admitted that the discovery of one or two more contemporary documents might be epoch-making: that even intrinsically insignificant records of that time might prove most significant in the sidelights they might throw on those which we already possess. Here it is, then, that the Franciscan parallel seems extraordinarily instructive. Numerous and comparatively recent as the Franciscan records are, there are lamentable gaps even here; but enough still remains to supply living and indisputable examples in the Franciscan scriptures of a process which we can only surmise as theoretically probable in the canonical scriptures.

St Francis died in the autumn of 1226: his *First Life* by Thomas of Celano was written at the bidding of Gregory IX in 1228 or 1229. Thomas, like Mark, was not himself one of the intimate disciples: he wrote admittedly from evidence supplied by others who had known the saint far better than he. Nearly twenty years later, in 1244, the general chapter of the order felt that still more ought to be formally recorded about their Founder before the first generation died away. Word was sent round, therefore, that all who possessed first-hand information should contribute it to the common stock; and Celano was again chosen to put this material into literary form. Those who responded most liberally to this circular were three of the saint's closest intimates, Leo, Angelo and Ruffino; what they had to say was written down by Leo, who had been St Francis's secretary. Leo's 'rolls' or 'papers,' as they are called by sub-contemporary witnesses, were partly used by Celano in compiling his *Second Life*; and Leo himself did, to some unspecified extent, collaborate with Celano in this work. In 1266, a step was taken which would be scarcely credible if it were not vouched for by such unexceptionable evidence. The general chapter of that year, under the presidency of St Bonaventura, decreed that St Bonaventura's own new *Life* of the Founder should henceforth be taken as the one authentic record, and that all earlier documents should be destroyed. This was done very thoroughly; the condemned records have survived in very few MSS, nearly all of which were preserved in out-of-the-way friaries. If the community had obeyed this order absolutely, the loss would have been irreparable; for St Bonaventura had never even seen his master except for one moment as a child of six, and his biography is not only far briefer than Celano's, but far more conventional, and even misleading on certain important points. Still more regrettable, perhaps, would have been the total loss of all Leo's other papers, apart from what Celano incorporated in his *Second Life*. These were kept for some time by the nuns of St Clare, and came afterwards into the hands of a man who championed Leo's views; for by that time, at the end of the thirteenth century, there was already almost a schism in the order. In 1318, Leo's papers were edited by an unknown friar, in a compilation which became known as the *Mirror of Perfection*. These Leo-papers, like St Mark's gospel, have certainly been retouched to some extent: the book contains one or two things which must have been written after Leo's death; and there is a good deal of controversy as to the extent of the liberties taken by this editor of 1318. About a dozen years later, a friar wrote in Latin the first half of the book generally called the *Little Flowers of St Francis*, of which we have no complete copy except in an Italian translation of about 1350. The original materials from which this book was compiled were probably roughly contemporary with, if not from the stock of, Brother Leo. Leo's papers have also probably been utilized in another compilation of questionable authenticity, the so-called *Life of St Francis by his Three Companions*, which we cannot trace back earlier than about 1330.

To all these must be added a few brief writings by St Francis himself (the remnants of a more considerable body which we know to have existed); several chronicles written within the order; and numerous brief references to him and his order by outside chroniclers and other witnesses, during or shortly after his lifetime. So far, this description of the Franciscan documents would be endorsed, I believe, by students of all schools, some of whom would dissent from the deductions which I now propose to draw.

You will see that the latest document here taken account of, the *Little Flowers*, dates from about 100 years after the saint's death, and therefore answers in point of time to the writer who added the ending of St Mark's gospel about a century after the crucifixion. And, in the far more numerous Franciscan documents, we have noted already some analogies with New Testament origins. Let us now consider these in much fuller detail.

The Franciscan documents present the following peculiarities—to use the word which comes most naturally to us now, though it really implies a very serious anachronism; for these characteristics, though to us they seem peculiarities, are simply normal in the history of the transmission of documents before the age of printing.

(1) *Carelessness of the written word.* The disciples were soaked through and through with St Francis, and through him with certain portions of gospel history; but this was mainly through oral tradition, since the large majority of

the first generation were illiterate. The idea of handing down written affidavits to posterity would have been among the last of their preoccupations. Though they did not live under the same daily and hourly expectation of the end of all things as Christ's first disciples, yet the middle ages in general were so convinced that the world was at its last gasp, and provision for a distant posterity was so alien to these men's ordinary habits, that most things were done with a hand-to-mouth carelessness which we find it difficult to conceive. A considerable fraction of St Francis's own writings, and probably the greater part, perished very early. None of the general chapter acts for the first thirty years have survived, though numerous official copies of these were almost certainly made for different friaries. Of Celano's third book, a collection of St Francis's miracles compiled at the express command of the minister general, one single MS is extant, which was only discovered and printed in our own day. Already in the fourteenth century, Celano's *Second Life* had almost perished, though it gives a far more personal picture of the Master than the first. It was evidently unknown to two out of the three most diligent Franciscan compilers of that century, and survives now in only two MSS, which differ greatly from each other. The priceless collection of anecdotes and sayings by Leo and his companions has been so mutilated and interpolated and scattered that room is left for very wide differences of opinion as to their historical value. A good deal of this, of course, is due to the decree of destruction in 1266; but (*a*) it is scarcely possible that St Francis's own writings, for instance, can have been deliberately destroyed under this decree; and (*b*) the very fact that such a decree was possible, under the leadership of St Bonaventura, who had been a distinguished professor of the greatest university in Europe, does but emphasize this characteristic carelessness with regard to documentary evidence. The Franciscans, although they possessed a

great convent at Assisi in which papal bulls and other
archives were stored, and though they were already further
organized and settled at St Francis's death than the
Christian community was at any time during the first two
centuries, did nevertheless show a neglect of the written
word, so far as their Founder's life and teaching were concerned, which we find a difficulty in realizing in spite of
the plainest documentary proofs. It may be added, however, that an exactly similar phenomenon has appeared in
our own day. A new religion, that of the Bábís, which
developed within the bosom of Mahomadanism, had for
its messiah one Mirza Ali, who, before his martyrdom in
1850, appointed Subh-i-Azal as his successor. After a
while, the leadership of the new religion was usurped
by Subh-i-Azal's half-brother and right-hand-man, Bahá-
ulláh. This man's followers succeeded in suppressing
almost completely the earliest and most authentic history
of the sect, of which only one perfect and one imperfect
MS are now known to exist. For this suppressed and
authentic narrative they substituted one of their own, the
so-called *New History*, in which, as Prof. Browne puts it,
'all references to Subh-i-Azal were eliminated or altered,
and other features regarded as undesirable were suppressed
or modified[19].' A new religion feels above all things that
its mission is not to write history, but to make history;
even where it most definitely claims the sanction of the
past, its true face is set most steadily towards the future.
'Let the dead bury their dead'; all minds will tend, even
unconsciously, to cast off so much of the past as is felt to
trammel present freedom; and, when once the religion is
organized, the temptation of the officials will be not only
to let the dead past bury itself, but to kill and bury so
much of it as is inconvenient for the present.

(2) In consequence of this, there is a terrible amount of
contamination (to use a technical word) among the sources.
It is practically agreed by all New Testament scholars that

some difficulties in the gospels are caused by scribes who have made notes and additions on the margin of the early MSS, and succeeding scribes who thrust those notes or additions into the text. A great deal of this was demonstrably done in the Franciscan documents; and many existing MSS are so contaminated as to be in reality compound MSS—here a bit of Celano, there a bit of Leo, then Celano again, then a page from some other source, and so on. Even university scholars in the middle ages, side by side with their frequent appeal to certain standard authors as almost inspired, failed, in the other half of their minds, to keep steadily in view the evidential value of an author's name. So long as a thing was written, they often cared comparatively little who wrote it. You must mentally underline that word 'steadily,' because there were exceptions which, as usual, swung into the other extreme. When a medieval scholar once realized the value of an author's name, he was not always scrupulous in using it; he would commend a book to the public under the name of some author who carried weight with everybody. For instance, if you look at any good modern edition of St Bonaventura or St Bernard, you will find that about 25 per cent. of what passed under those names in the later middle ages is spurious.

(3) Nor can it be said that men were cruel only to the body of the MSS (so to speak), but faithful to their spirit; that they were true to the essential reality, and neglectful only of its formal outward trappings. Medieval writers aimed far less at history than at edification. If a learned pope, and then the chapter general, chose Celano rather than Leo to write the official lives of St Francis, this was not because Celano knew one-tenth of what Leo did, but because he was a scholar and a rhetorician, who would trick the story out to their taste. If, again, Celano was superseded by the still more official Bonaventura, this was because Bonaventura was not only a more accomplished

scholar and rhetorician, but also (in the jargon of theological partisans) a 'safe man.'

(4) For (and this brings me to my fourth point, which
I must emphasize in the next lecture) there were parties in
the order even before the Founder's death; and it mattered
very much to the official class whether St Francis were
described by their party or by another. Angelo Clareno,
a younger contemporary of St Bonaventura, tells us plainly
why that destruction of 1266 had been decreed. Writing
about 1320, he complains that much early evidence had
already passed into oblivion, 'partly because all things
that had been written in the *First Legend* were cancelled
and destroyed at the bidding of Brother Bonaventura
when he had written his own new *Life of St Francis*, and
partly because they were despised, since they seemed contrary to the common course, [i.e. of life in our order].'
Angelo was a man who lived many years in imminent
danger of death at the hands of his fellow-Franciscans for
his inconvenient zeal in clinging to what he believed to be
the primitive ideal of St Francis; therefore from him and
from his friends we cannot expect complete impartiality
either. Hence nine-tenths of the surviving records of
St Francis's life are, to some extent, partisan documents;
and they must be read from that point of view. In every
case, allowance must be made for what we know to be the
author's tendency.

(5) This brings me to my last point. There was one
tendency common to them all—the laudable desire to
exalt their hero. Even their intestine quarrels would impel
them to vie all the more with each other in praise of the
man to whose example and authority each party professed-
ly appealed. There is, therefore, a generally progressive
tendency to forget the little human weaknesses which
(though they endear St Francis all the more to the modern
mind, and, showing us the real man more clearly, heighten
the moral miracle of his life in the judgment of most candid

readers) were ill suited to that far more conventional
picture of the saint which the authorities would be naturally anxious to display. Therefore, although Leo's frank
naturalism is a reaction against the comparatively conventional Celano, and though the *Little Flowers*, again, are
full of the earlier and more human touches, yet the authors
in both these cases were of the spiritual party—the party
which the decree of destruction was designed to silence—
and certainly the records in general lose these human
touches more and more as time wears on. The growing
apotheosis of the founder proceeds on conventional
medieval lines; that is, through a crescendo of the miraculous. The multiplicity of Franciscan documents enables
us to trace here, even more clearly than in many other
parallel cases, the progressive stress laid on the hero's
miraculous powers. The farther we get from those who
knew him as a living man, the deeper we find him buried
in these marvels.

We have seen already how Jordan of Giano, who knew
St Francis personally, confesses to having given the living
saint less credit for miracles than he gave after death to
his relics. Celano and Leo, who also knew the living
Francis, are among the very soberest of medieval hagio-
graphers; we have seen how Celano felt to owe his readers
an apology on that score. But, before Celano died, he was
called upon to produce a separate *Book of Miracles*; and
the tide rose until it reached its extreme possible limit—
in 1399, a century and three quarters after the saint's
death—in Bartholomew of Pisa's *Book of Conformities*.
This bulky compilation, designed to show how exactly
Francis followed Christ, proves also (if we take it seriously)
that immeasurably more miracles are recorded of him than
of his Master. In his 39th *Fructus* Bartholomew relates
thirty cases of dead folk raised to life by St Francis,
living or canonized. A selection from this book was published by the reformers in Holland, with ribald comments,

under the title of *The Koran of the Cordeliers*. It is illustrated with copper-plates; and, the more faithfully these
follow Bartholomew's text, the more cruelly they carica-
ture the real Francis of Assisi.

Let me conclude this evening with the history of the
most famous of all Franciscan miracles, which may serve
to support my contention that, while we may often trust
ancient documents to show us the real soul of a man, we
cannot rely upon them for that precision of detail, and that
scientific anticipation of natural objections, which alone
can beat down the suspense of judgment which every man
morally owes, *a priori*, in face of a miraculous claim.
I allude to the famous history of the stigmata—the five
wounds of Christ alleged to have been miraculously impressed upon St Francis's body. I regret that time allows
me only to give the briefest sketch here.

In this case, for once, we have a document even earlier
and more trustworthy than the exceptionally early and
trustworthy Celano. From the strictly historical point of
view—for you will permit me to remind you here, for the
last time, that history is bound to aim at controlling all
recorded evidence with that scientific accuracy which
nobody dreams of omitting in a laboratory or in a work-
shop—from the scientific and historical point of view,
there is no Christian miracle of equal importance so well
attested as this. We have here, for once, something that
does really resemble an affidavit. Brother Elias was St
Francis's official representative, and had acted as head of
the order during these last months. This Brother Elias,
then, within a few hours of the Founder's death, sent
round an official circular to the provincial heads of the
order[20]. He has, he says, a new and unheard-of event to
relate. 'Not long before his death our Brother and Father
appeared as crucified, bearing in his body five wounds
which are in truth the marks of Christ; for his hands and
feet had as it were the punctures of nails; which [punc-

tures] were pierced on both sides, disclosing scars and showing the blackness of iron. But his side appeared lanced, and often exuded blood.' As I am asking you to look very closely into these words, I will read them again.

Now, you will note that the actual appearances for which Elias can vouch are very simple. There were wounds of some sort at the five crucial spots, more or less scarred over. And the wounds showed *nigredinem ferri*, 'the blackness of iron,' or 'of the iron.' I assume that there is no exaggeration in these words of Elias; still less should I dream of supposing, as Renan does, conscious deception. Renan, I must frankly say, seems here to fall into that vulgar error which is even less respectable, perhaps, than superstition—the vulgar error of baseless scepticism. This description of 'as it were the punctures of nails, which punctures were pierced on both sides, disclosing scars and showing the blackness of iron,' would be satisfied by any amorphous wound, scarcely more than skin-deep on either side, with a dark core in the midst. We know that the saint, during all the last years of his life, was in a state of bodily sickness mainly induced by persistent fasting, over-work and want of sleep. He wore no linen, but only the coarsest of woollen stuffs, and seldom washed; from an ascetic sense of duty, he lived habitually as our soldiers are often compelled to live in the trenches. Elias says himself: 'While the breath yet lived in his body, there was no beauty in him, but his face was despised, and not a limb of his body remained without exceeding pain.' We have explicit testimony, in one of the stigmata anecdotes themselves, that he sometimes begged his friends to scratch him—a friendly office which is common in Italy even at the present day [21]. We know, again, that he was increasingly and increasingly possessed with the ideal of imitating his master Christ, and especially, in later years, his master's bodily sufferings. In those long nights of ecstasy and half-delirium of which we hear, when his whole being was concentrated on the contemplation of Christ's wounds, he might quite naturally and unconsciously finger his own hands and feet and side, where all his thoughts were fixed. Thus, in fingering and fingering, he would irritate the already irritable skin; then, the more the irritation grew, he would naturally touch it all the more frequently and unconsciously. Nobody who has had to do with children can have failed to remark how difficult it is to keep their fingers from a sore—how unconsciously they often touch it—and how grown-up people, also, are frequently victims of this unconscious habit. I cannot help thinking that these perfectly natural possibilities would fully account for all that Elias can vouch for seeing. No judge in court, I am convinced, would venture to interpret his written words further than that. If counsel should plead: 'But this affidavit says distinctly *the blackness of iron*,' then the obvious answer would be: 'Blackness he *saw*; iron he *supposed*. Who could tell, without minute examination and various tests, whether the blackness in the centre of a wound were caused by a rusty nail or by any other of a hundred possible discolorations? And what evidence have we that any such examination was undertaken by this witness, who betrays no sense even of the importance of the distinction?' Would not any judge be careful to warn the jury that, if they convicted a prisoner on the strength of this word *iron*, they would be convicting him on a mere unsupported hypothesis. Moreover, even contemporaries seem to have hesitated far more than we should have expected. It is not only that rival Religious, such as the Dominicans, persistently denied this miracle almost to the end of the thirteenth century. The pope himself, who, as cardinal Ugolino, had known St Francis so long and so intimately, did not insert any reference to this 'new and unheard of' miracle in the bull of canonization; and though, nine years later, he defended it and laid great stress upon it, yet those nine years had brought such temptations to conformity with a now established tradition that this later pronouncement cannot really counterbalance his earlier silence. Moreover, St Bonaventura and the *Little Flowers* tell us that he doubted for some time of the wound in the side—though Elias's letter vouches for this as plainly as for the rest, and historically speaking the evidence is distinctly stronger for it than for the others. And, almost as significant, we find very soon that Elias's affidavit is not considered sufficient by the upholders of the miracle, who set to work to improve upon it. Already in Celano's first life the wounds with their vague 'blackness of iron' have become something very much more definite and extraordinary. 'His hands and feet seemed pierced in the midst by nails, the heads of the nails appearing in the inner part of the hands and in the upper part of the feet, and their points over against them. Now those marks were round on the inner side of the hands and elongated on the other side, and certain small pieces of flesh were seen like the ends of nails bent and driven back, projecting from the rest of the flesh. So also the marks of nails were imprinted in his feet, and raised above the rest of the flesh. Moreover his right side, as if it had been pierced by a lance, was overlaid with a scar, and often shed forth blood, so that his tunic and drawers were many times sprinkled with the sacred blood [22].' St Bonaventura, of course, takes care to describe them no less miraculously than Celano. And later again, in the *Little Flowers*, part of the story of the stigmata is written frankly, like many other such stories in the middle ages, from revelation [23]. A pious friar doubts as to certain particulars, he prays for a revelation; this is vouchsafed in a vision, and the fresh details thus supplied are put down as history. But such incidents as this, while they can bring to our minds no real corroboration of the miracle, are proof positive that the early Franciscans felt the evidence to be unsatisfactorily scanty. And to the very last, I believe, medieval painters and sculptors never got beyond Elias's voucher; I have been able neither to see nor to hear of any medieval representation of the nails with their heads and points as described by Celano and Bonaventura[24].

There is equal doubt, again, as to the time when these wounds appeared. Elias's 'not long before,' which is very strongly corroborated by outside evidence, seems quite inconsistent with the version afterwards universally received, that the stigmata were miraculously impressed upon St Francis's body *two years* before his death. And yet this latter tradition has the express support of Brother Leo, our only other direct first-hand witness. Again, as to the way in which St Francis managed to conceal them, or how far he did conceal them during these two years, there are very serious difficulties in the evidence, and such as might prove quite fatal in a modern law-court[25].

While regretting to deal so briefly with a complicated and most interesting problem, I hope that even these scanty details will be found to support my main contention of this evening. A document may be of the greatest spiritual value, and yet almost worthless as historical evidence for physical miracles. Indeed, even the directest and precisest of ancient or medieval documents—even Elias's circular letter, which is almost unparalleled in earlier hagiography—would not go far if we relied upon that alone, or even mainly upon that. We must make this distinction, or else give up our religious faith as soon as we begin to enter seriously upon the study of history. If religion is to be bound up inextricably with the belief that it is possible to find fourteen verses in St Mark which have the evidential value of a legal affidavit, then religion must fall; the man from the trenches will no longer be persuaded so to shut his eyes. We live in a better world than those primitive centuries in which such a confusion of ideas could reign undisturbed over men's minds. If, on the other hand, with Origen and St Augustine and St Gregory, we lay our main stress upon the moral miracle of Christianity, then we are safe so long as Christianity remains, what it certainly now is, a beacon to humanity. If Christianity ever ceased to be this good deed shining in a naughty world, then, I suppose, it would go: but then I suppose it ought to go. Meanwhile we are safe enough here, and may boldly face the fact (which in any case we could not escape) that, while we may rely upon the gospels for religious essentials, we cannot implicitly trust them for those physical miracles which the best minds have relegated to the secondary place. Wherever faith requires a real effort, we believe Mark's word only because we believe *in* Christ; and we are constrained to believe Mark only so far as the belief in Christ necessarily involves such credit. Even those who believe that they are believing an affidavit, would pay very little heed to similar affidavits about anyone else. They too, unconsciously to themselves, believe Mark's word because they believe in Christ.

If there be any here who cling to the confusion between two lines of evidence which really run on different planes, and who feel that they cannot in their own minds suspend judgment to wait for further proof of a single miracle in St Mark, lest they should lose altogether their faith in Christ, to such I would quote what Renan says in his essay on St Francis: 'Nous avons la preuve que, sauf les circonstances miraculeuses, le caractère réel de François d'Assise répond exactement au portrait qui est resté de lui. François d'Assise a toujours été une des raisons les plus fortes qui m'ont fait croire que Jésus fut à peu près tel que les évangélistes synoptiques nous le dépeignent[26].'

# IV

IN my first lecture, I pleaded that we should not deny the name of Christian to any follower of Christ. In the second, it was necessary to plead for a far greater concession; that the question of what St Gregory calls corporeal miracles should be so far subordinated to the spiritual miracle of Christianity as to remove one of the most important obstacles to religious unity. In the third, it became necessary to distinguish between purely historical grounds for belief in physical miracles (which in the nature of the case must be slight) and moral grounds, which are certainly much stronger, but on the other hand much more subjective; so that our own personal belief gives us much less justification for insisting, as a primary condition of fellowship, that others should believe with us. Here, again, there seems a reason for suspension of judgment, if only in the spirit in which trade-unionists have suspended theirs. But you will see that, hitherto, I have pleaded only with each individual, asking him to make these concessions out of individual charity, if not as a matter of individual necessity. To this, however, it may be answered, and very truly answered: 'We are not merely individuals, we are part of a church. Just as we are necessarily forbidden, for reasons of higher national interest, to make individually what might otherwise be harmless concessions to individual Germans, so also, until the church and the world have fought out their long fight, the church justly forbids us to fraternize with the world on the basis of any concession of principle, however momentary or conditional.' If the parallel were complete, I for one should be inclined to give a great deal of weight to this objection. No collective action or thought can be fruitful without some degree of discipline; we need not

only to attract the multitude, but also to get some coherence among the multitude; and such coherence postu-
lates to some extent the sacrifice of individual inclination.
But, in this particular case, I will ask you to join with me
now in scrutinizing the claims of authority. We are willing
to defer to the British government, as represented by the
police or even by the special constable; but we may lawfully ask first to see the constable's badge. Where is the
church's clear mark of authority here? Is there really any
existing body which has the right to forbid, and which does
actually forbid, our even suspending our judgment for a
while on these contentious questions with which I have
dealt? God, unquestionably, has supreme authority even
over our inmost conscience: but has he deputed that
authority to any body to whose voice we may listen in the
certain assurance that it is God's voice?

You have seen, to begin with, that this supposed prohibition of reconsidering the miracle question was far from
absolute, even in the days when ecclesiastical discipline
was most despotic both in theory and in practice. The
middle ages were not always so hopelessly medieval as
they are sometimes pictured. Even if we had no more to
rely upon than this, and than the actual statements of
principle from St Augustine and St Gregory which I have
quoted, these alone would seem to indicate one clear conclusion—that the best men even of the middle ages permitted this latitude—we may say more, *claimed* this
latitude—because they felt they would otherwise risk
bringing Christianity into conflict with plain reason. These
men were willing to raise dogma *above* reason to an indefinite extent; but they did all they could to avoid committing themselves to anything that is simply *against*
reason; to anything that is contradicted by that plain
sense which guides our daily life, and which Christ himself
so often addressed.

But, as students of history, we have what seems a

simpler answer still. We may doubt whether there exists now, or ever has existed, a clear-cut teaching and commanding Christian church in the sense in which there exists a clear-cut, teaching and commanding British state. If we are to accept the parallel of a state at all, must we not say that the story of the Christian church is rather the story of the present Russian state?—of a constant struggle for power between rival elements, and the same difficulty in finding unquestionable ecclesiastical authority now, after 1900 years, as in deciding who is really speaking for the millions of Russia—Bolshevik, Menschevik, Cadet or Imperialist? The fact that one section of Christians—the Roman Catholic—puts forward the clearest and most exclusive claims of all, and that the governors of this church have never yet repudiated their ancient official pretensions to crush all opposition by fire and sword—that fact proves no more, in itself, than the fact that a modern Bolshevik is equally convinced, equally exclusive, and equally willing to reconcile his theoretical charity for all mankind with the practical use of a revolver shooting at sight. The claims of rival churches cannot all be true; but they may all be partly true: in this conflict, therefore, the natural arbiter would seem to be history.

Here we stand at a fortunate moment. Eight years ago, Canon J. M. Wilson preached at Cambridge a university sermon in which he appealed for a fresh examination of the historical basis of the Roman catholic and Anglo-catholic theories of church privileges and apostolical succession. His age, his experience, his intellectual distinction gave him every right to issue this appeal, and the late Professor Swete, recognizing this, chose six distinguished scholars to co-operate in such an examination. The results were published a few months ago under the title of *The Early History of the Church and the Ministry*. The welcome already extended to this imposing volume authorizes us to take it as representing the cream of what has been worked out in Britain on this subject during all these centuries. The terms of reference were that the authors should write from the historical point of view; and from that standpoint they must be judged. I propose to confine myself mainly to the first three essays, entitled *Early Conceptions of the Church, The Apostolic Ministry* and *Apostolic Succession*. These, the most relevant to our purpose, fill 214 octavo pages; and, coming as they do in direct answer to Canon Wilson's detailed and searching questions, we must take them as professing to offer us a handbook of church constitutional history during, roughly, the first three centuries and a half of Christendom.

Let any student turn from a book on secular English or French or German constitutional history to these 214 pages, and he will be struck first of all, I think, by the extraordinary vagueness of definition among our three church historians. It may almost be said that the essence of a good constitutional history is clear definition. It may be said equally truly that the writers in Dr Swete's volume seem to avoid definition almost as deliberately as other historians catch at it. Yet the need is even greater in ecclesiastical than in secular history. During eighteen at least out of these nineteen Christian centuries, men have discussed with extreme eagerness the real meaning of the words *church, ministry* and *succession*. Thousands, it may be literally said, have shed their blood for one definition or another. Yet here in 1918, in answer to a special appeal for clear information, from a distinguished churchman who emphasized the growing danger of this continued confusion, we are still left in the dark, or in twilight at the very best. If we cannot blame the three authors for this—and I, for one, feel that this hesitation to define is in many ways an indication of their breadth of view and their true sense of history—if, then, we cannot attribute this vagueness to the authors, we are all the more compelled to attribute it to the very nature of their task. St Augustine, a man of

commanding genius, standing very near those sources of
oral tradition on which such stress is often laid, failed
signally here. His argument is constantly confused between different conceptions of the church, it even depends,
one might almost say, on such confusions. The present
bishop of Oxford, who for combined learning and piety
has no superior in the Anglican church, published two
years ago a little book called *The Religion of the Church, a
Manual of Membership*, of which 20,000 copies were sold
in four months. I think I am right in saying that the
author commits himself to no definition of the crucial word
*church*. We are to listen and to obey, but to whom must
we listen, and whom obey?. The bishop of Oxford, or the
bishop of Hereford? or, again, the verdict of a united
episcopate, which has so little existence in fact that the
whole Anglican bench of a century ago would have condemned both Oxford and Hereford; and that the whole
bench of a century hence may conceivably find both of
them too conservative? Of course, Roman catholic
definition is clear enough; but it violates plain facts of
history. Many Anglo-catholics think they have defined it
when they say with St Vincent of Lérins that the church
is the body of Catholics, and that things catholie are things
which have been held *semper, ubique, ab omnibus*—always,
everywhere, and by all Christians. But this, again, is
absolutely unhistorical; there is scarcely anything which
can claim this title to catholicity in any real sense. Even
the doctrine of the Trinity, for instance, was really an open
question for three centuries; however commonly the words
*God* and *divine* may have been used, they meant very different things to different minds[27]. Many tenets repudiated by
the so-called catholic churches have been held by large
numbers who have steadily claimed church membership.
It is true, the majorities have thrust them forth, and often
persecuted them until they accepted the fact of separation.
But there is no proof here of a divine commission; all we

can here see is the force of a majority. Even where the separatists have been eliminated very differently, by force of argument, we have here nothing directly and clearly divine. Argument is not infallible; the arguments by which the Mosaic authorship of the pentateuch was established to the full conviction of most churchmen a hundred years ago are now abandoned by all. No appeal to majorities can finally help us; we are still left seeking for such an authority, directly binding on the conscience, as would have a clear right to forbid our making concessions to other parties for the sake of a greater agreement among professing Christians.

The problem, in fact, lies deeper than any of Professor Swete's collaborators would lead us to realize; and here, I think, we cannot altogether acquit them. The root-question is one which they never state explicitly enough, and never seem fully to face. Did Christ give to his disciples, and leave to posterity, plain instructions about church membership and church authority? Did he define clearly to the apostles, or give them clear power to define (a) who is in the church and who out, or (b) who has authority to teach, and who must content himself with listening and obeying? Did Christ prescribe these things clearly, if not in detail, at least in such full and cogent general principles as could leave room for no honest doubt among his followers? Or, on the other hand, did he leave the question to his followers to solve in their own consciences under God, as he left John Baptist's disciples to solve the yet more fundamental question of his Messiahship, so that the modern Quaker's answer, and the Roman catholic's answer, must alike be judged by their fruits? This question is so obvious, and so fundamental, that no discussion of those three words *church, ministry* and *succession* which does not begin by stating it clearly, and which does not keep it clearly in the reader's view all along, can be called thoroughly satisfactory. It is not invidious to express the opinion that the best of these essays is the third, by Mr Turner. But even Mr Turner's learning, while it has added greatly to our detailed knowledge of the early evidence, scarcely brings Christians nearer to a practical solution than 200 years ago; indeed, scarcely to any nearer agreement on principle than what we seem able to trace in apostolic times. Meanwhile, the want of agreement is fatal. Only the other day, this was put with great force from the University pulpit. 'We are met with endless discussion,' said the preacher, 'as to what the church is, and whether this religious body or that religious individual is a part of it [28].' This being so—and we all know how true it is—we naturally expect that no preacher should argue from so dubious a word without first defining the sense in which he himself uses it. Yet in this case, as in others, no definition was attempted; and we were warned·with the usual emphasis and reiteration to regulate our lives by the 'authority' and the 'teaching voice' of a body so indefinite that no man can be certain where and when it speaks, or with what authority. Moreover, even the Roman church is, at bottom, almost as dubious. She takes care that there shall not be, within her jurisdiction, these endless discussions as to what she is or who are her subjects; yet, behind this mask of certainty, we find the same fundamental uncertainties. There is a startling instance of this in one of the greatest of the great Bossuet's sermons— that on the Eminent Dignity of the Poor in the Church. Without giving the least hint that he is using the word in any transcendental sense—clearly implying, on the contrary, that he speaks, as usual, of the visible church— Bossuet spends all his time in attributing characteristics to her which are ludicrously false of any body that has called itself church for the last fifteen centuries, at least. 'Even as it is the poor who possess heaven, that kingdom of God in eternity, so it is they also who possess the church, that kingdom of God in this world.... Providence gives to

the poor the first places in the church, a rank so privileged
that the rich are admitted into the church only on condition of serving the poor'...and so on. All through that
splendid sermon—for splendid it is, with all its faults—
Bossuet is simply juggling with the two different conceptions of *church visible* and *church invisible*, which are
in fact as remote from each other as the actual British
Empire is from the ideal League of Nations [29]. We are obliged
to pardon even the greatest religious writers who trade
upon this confusion of terms; for few have altogether
avoided it. But who would pardon a secular writer who
introduced the same confusion into worldly politics? Even
though there were no other evidence, would not this constant confusion between different senses of the word
*church*, from the very earliest times to the present day,
seem almost conclusive against the theory that church is
as definite a thing as state, and that Christianity began
with a clear teaching of the Holy Spirit on this point?
The state, when it commands our obedience, speaks with
one certain voice, and defines clearly who are subject to
her authority, who are exempt. Why should the church
alone persist in claiming our submission to that which she
herself shrinks from defining? And why should not Christians agree to use the word ordinarily in that sense in
which Bossuet really uses it when he speaks of the eminent
dignity of the poor? Why should not the church mean all
who really try to follow Christ, and the voice of the church
be what all these men and women have to teach us? Yes,
and even more; for the church in this highest and widest
sense did not begin with Christ's mission on earth; it was
already there in embryo, in that Law which he declared
that he was come not to destroy but to fulfil. In that sense,
we may appeal to men to listen to a church which no man
can define, even as we claim obedience for a God whom no
man can define; in each case, the power to which we appeal
is too great and too living for definition in words; each

c.

man must arrive at an approximate definition in his own conscience. In this case we are confronted, not with a power of the same kind as the state, strong in its officialism and clear in its commands, but with something less tangible in proportion as it is greater—with the whole sum-total of God's working in the human soul through the agency of all other human beings who have, in any degree, a message of God for that soul. If this be the true church, then St Paul was not disobedient to the church when, after his conversion, he 'conferred not with flesh and blood, neither went up to Jerusalem to them which were apostles before him' (Gal. i. 16, 17); nor are we so disobedient when, in our own conscience before God, we are compelled to reject some point taught by ecclesiastical officials, in favour of the contrary opinion of some quite unofficial seeker after God. Our church education, on these terms, differs not in kind but only in degree from God's ordinary education of the human race, wherein he puts before us daily and hourly, in the secret of our own souls, the alternatives of good and evil, and we learn, by our own open-eyed and deliberate choice, daily and hourly more about God and ourselves. But in that case (it may be objected to us), God only knows whether you are listening to the church's voice or not. True; but God does know, and that is enough. Here, at least, is a clear and consistent principle, the final responsibility of each soul to its Creator only, however much it may also owe to its fellow-men. Short of this, as it seems to me, we wander without principle; and the very men who most precisely insist on our obedience to the church, are least able to give a working definition of the church which we are to obey. Meanwhile, millions of Christians are separated from each other by this continued disagreement as to membership and teaching authority. How much longer are we to wait for a practical solution? Are we to wait another 1900 years? I cannot help thinking that the learned vagueness of scholars such as Mr Turner

and his fellow-labourers—a vagueness strictly commensurate with their learning, since an Irish peasant would cut
the knot in a single word—creates a very strong presumption that Christ laid down no clear rule on these points,
but meant us to work out our own salvation.

Even comparatively conservative scholars are willing
now to admit that he may have been long in great doubt
about his own Messiahship; and again, that his expectation
of an immediate end to this present world may have put
it out of the question that he should have arranged with
his disciples for a succession which, *ex hypothesi*, could not
be foreseen. You will find this hinted, though scarcely put
into its logical place, on p. 4 of the first essay in Dr Swete's
volume; and, if you read carefully the succeeding paragraph, verifying the references, I think most of you will
feel with me that the author's very cursory treatment of
this fundamental point weakens the whole framework of
his essay. The Pauline authorship of the epistle to the
Ephesians, for instance, is treated in this paragraph as
unquestioned: but the second essayist, on p. 65, very
properly reminds us that there is room for legitimate
doubts on the point. There is much more doubt as to the
genuineness of certain texts in St Matthew's gospel; and
this our essayists recognize, declining therefore to build
upon them. Apart from these doubtful verses of St Matthew, and from the historically still less certain fourth
gospel, there seems to be nothing in the gospels which even
professes to give direct evidence that our Lord ever contemplated a church, in anything like the sense postulated
by those who would tell us that the authority of the church
deprives us now of any moral right to suspend our judgment on the subject of physical miracles. Nor can any
such church be got out of the epistle to the Ephesians, nor
even, I think, out of the pastoral epistles, which again our
essayists recognize to be as doubtful as the fourth gospel
or the disputed passages in Matthew. In the whole New

Testament, then, there is no evidence which an outsider, looking at the question without prepossessions, would treat as sufficient; while, against the theory, we have such strong indications as the answer to John Baptist's disciples, and the rebuke to St John for his uncharitable prohibition of the well-doer who 'followeth not with us[30].'

Take again the history of the word *catholic*. This word, which is Greek for *universal*, does not even profess to be biblical; it has not even the dubious authority of a suspected interpolation; it first occurs in St Ignatius, two generations after Christ's death. At that time (we are told by the first essayist on pp. 24 and 438) the church was called 'catholic, because extending to all mankind.' But it never has extended to all mankind nor anything like all—an elementary and obvious difficulty which the writer makes no attempt to meet[31]. We hope this extension will come some day; but, when that time comes, we may be sure that the authority of the church will no longer be questioned. Meanwhile, unfortunately, its authority is very seriously questioned; and it would seem suicidal to base our claim to authority upon an alleged status which, upon direct challenge, we are compelled to admit we have not yet reached, even after the struggles of 1900 years. One of the first tasks of the historian is to realize how loosely terms were used in the unscientific past; and, if St Ignatius had really meant to assert by his use of *catholic* that the church extended to all mankind, we could only acquit him morally by pleading in his favour an almost incredible ignorance of fact. What he really meant was what the word certainly connoted later on, as the essayist himself explains, writing on the same page 24: 'In its later sense [the word *catholic*], as a fixed attitude, implies orthodoxy as opposed to heresy, conformity as opposed to dissent.' Now, this is sheer *majoritarianism*, if I may so coin a name for the doctrine that majorities are always in the right. No doubt majorities *are* generally right in a rough way: that is the fundamental principle of democracy, and in practical life it works as well as other similar principles. But we know that it would be fatal to apply it strictly to the realm of intellect and conscience. We know that, though the majority of society may legitimately do what it can to silence a dissentient member for a time and under special circumstances, yet it is not legitimate to suppress his views altogether by death or perpetual imprisonment, since we all recognize that he may just conceivably be in the right, even though he be in a minority of one. The very strictest state-disciplinarians, now-a-days, would recognize this as a conceivable possibility. Even Bolsheviks would generally recognize it. If they claim the right to kill socialists less numerous than themselves, it only is because they are convinced that, in this deadly crisis, they cannot safely suffer these dissentients to survive on the mere off-chance of their proving to be in the right. But even Bolsheviks would admit this off-chance, and would not base themselves deliberately on a theory of the eternal infallibility of majorities in the intellectual, moral or religious sphere. Yet this is what we are asked to do when we are told to submit our thoughts to the church because she is catholic, and when her catholicity is demonstrated by her majoritarianism. The whole of this section of the essay, you will probably feel, is vitiated by the failure to recognize that majoritarianism is an excellent practical rule, but a very bad substitute in spiritual matters for such a clear divine mandate as is assumed in the theory that our consciences are absolutely subjected to the church.

Passing on next to the question of the ministry, I think you will find the arguments in Dr Swete's volume equally inconclusive. You will find some sort of ministry very early in existence; though its changes are apparently rapid and kaleidoscopic. You will find it at a very early stage claiming to represent the Founder; and, as time goes on,

you will find its claims growing clearer and clearer, its
delimitations from the laity more and more definite[32].
But, as you read, ask yourself at every sentence: 'Is there
here anything more than man, with his social and orderly
instincts, would naturally evolve for himself, under such
an impulse of faith and under such feelings of brotherhood
and moral responsibility as the disciples certainly inherited from Christ? Is there, in short, any proof in this
volume that Christ prescribed more plainly on this subject
than he did to John Baptist's disciples about his Messiahship? or that he did not deliberately leave his followers to
work out their own salvation under the impulse that he
had supplied?' I feel confident of the answer most of you
would find here in your own minds. And I think that
answer would be even more definite when you had come
to the end of the third essay—the ablest and most learned,
if that comparison be not invidious, in the whole book.

The author, Mr C. H. Turner, writes on the *Apostolic
Succession*, which is of course bound up with the ministra-
tion of the sacraments. The theory of apostolic succession
has been diversely stated and defined, though there is
much less vagueness about it than about different definitions of the church. As a matter of fact, nearly everyone would so define it as to limit the teaching church, and
the dispensation of the sacraments in general, to a small
minority of Christians. These (the theory assumes) have
received a special gift of the Holy Spirit which alone can
ensure the truth of their teaching and the validity of certain sacraments which they administer. This divine gift
they have received from Christ through the apostles, in a
direct line, by the laying on of hands. Nothing can fully
make up for the absence of this genuine apostolic ordination, in legitimate succession from the very first. Through
it, the church is infallible; while Christ-worshippers outside this system are subject to every possibility of error.
If this theory be true, it follows that these apostolic

successors have an official right to forbid our making the
concessions which I have asked you—and which, indeed,
it is the whole object of these lectures to ask you—to make
to your fellow-Christians.

But *is* the theory true? Mr Turner, though he defines
much more carefully than his two predecessors and concludes with nearly twenty closely-printed pages devoted
to the original sources, seems to leave us after all just
where our Lord's answer left the disciples of John the
Baptist[33]. Many readers will see in this a strong testimonial to his historical sense; but it is certainly not what
the ordinary theory of apostolic succession demands. If
that momentous claim be justified, how can the historian's
vagueness of conclusion be commensurate with his scientific eminence? The claim is clear enough; why then is all
the evidence that can be raked together in its support,
from nineteen centuries of Christian history, so inconclusive?

Let me first indicate one or two obvious objections to the
theory, which (as we had better begin by reminding ourselves again) is bound up with the catholic theory of the
sacraments. It assumes almost as a necessary consequence
that, even as Christ determined how the priest should be
marked off visibly from the laity, so also he instituted
certain sacraments for the priest to administer, whereof
one at least is essential to salvation, while all are of the
highest spiritual importance. The two theories go closely
together; and, if the sacraments are found to be vague and
uncertain, much of this uncertainty must recoil also upon
the sacramental ministry.

Here, then, the first striking fact is that orthodoxy has
not yet fully made up its mind, even at the present day,
as to the number of Christian sacraments. The Roman
catholic church has no doubt that there are seven, neither
more nor less, though she did not arrive at this certitude
until the end of the twelfth century after Christ. The

Greek church recognizes the same number, but more dubiously, having in fact adopted the Roman calculation, partly under compulsion, a century later[34]. The Anglo-catholics often accept this number also; for the Prayer-Book Catechism, though naming only two, is so phrased that, by reading between the lines, we may reconcile its wording with any number, a hundred or a thousand, without being accused of violating its plain sense. And if you answer here that the truth is probably on the side of the man who will give you the most positive answer, the Roman catholic, then you will be disconcerted to find that the Roman church never discovered marriage to be a sacrament until many centuries after she had put forth the claim to govern and teach all Christendom; and that, in the ages when she most insisted on its sacramental character, she did a great deal to rob it of sacramental respect. Not only in the middle ages, but far beyond, a boy of 14 and a girl of 12 might contract a valid marriage within the Roman communion, without priest and even without witnesses, by a simple exchange of verbal assurances. 'I take thee for my wife'—'I take thee for my husband' were the sacramental words which, once pronounced, bound them indissolubly to each other for the rest of their lives. And (to fill this cup of irreverence to the very brim) it was notorious that the rich and powerful were very unlucky if they could not get the church to divorce them at any time—to unsacrament this sacrament —under pretext of nullity of marriage. Henry VIII would not have had the least difficulty with Catharine of Aragon if she had not been aunt to the most powerful prince in Europe.

Again, you will find still more striking examples among the last fifty-three pages of Mr Turner's essay, in the section entitled *The Problem of Non-Catholic Orders*. Already in the third century, the most authoritative theologians contradicted each other as to that one sacra-

ment which the orthodox have always held as necessary
to salvation—the sacrament of baptism. Could baptism
be validly administered by an unorthodox Christian?
St Cyprian said *No*, St Augustine said *Yes*. But how is
this conflict of opinion reconcilable with the doctrine of
apostolic succession, unless we so whittle that doctrine
down as to divest it of all practical·significance? Our Lord,
it is assumed, had instituted a clear and elaborate system
to preserve the purity of sacramental administration; yet
here is the blackness of abysmal doubt in the catholic
church as to the one most essential sacrament of all. Two
words at the time of institution would have excluded to
all eternity any possibility of error on this point; why had
not these two words been pronounced to the disciples, any
more than the one conclusive word *Yes* had been given to
John the Baptist? Because, if we are to believe Mr Turner
on p. 143, 'this question, like all other questions of theory,
was not consciously formulated till the pressure of circumstances compelled churchmen to try to think out the
answer.' This can scarcely be accepted, even ·as a statement of probable historical fact, without considerable
reservation. Is it not most likely, on the contrary, that
sporadic cases of difficulty arose in the very first years or
even months of Christianity, and that St Cyprian was not
the first bishop puzzled by them, but only the first bishop
who had to face the problem on a great scale? for in his
case the salvation or damnation of whole populations was
at stake. Again, even if we accept Mr Turner's explanation
as an historical fact, how does it meet the obvious difficulty,
that this confessed uncertainty seems to rob apostolical
succession of all practical efficacy? The definite divinely-
appointed guardians of a definite, divinely-appointed and
essential sacrament could do nothing but contradict each
other. In the end, St Augustine's view prevailed, but,
meanwhile, generations had lived and died in different
parts of Christendom under a cloud of complete uncer-

tainty, if it be true that certainty can come only from the
decisions of apostolic successors. Baptism was an essential
to salvation; the unbaptized must go to hell, and meanwhile thousands died without knowing whether they were
baptized. Even on Mr Turner's plea (I say it with all
reverence), it is difficult to find the work of the Holy Spirit
here. Should we acquit even an ordinary statesman who,
in drafting a law of conveyance or inheritance, failed to
insert just two words prescribing whether the necessary
legal registration must be done before a government official,
or whether it would be quite valid if written and signed by
any citizen, male or female? 'On what plea, then' (we
must say to the Roman catholic or Anglo-catholic), 'can
you defend the blindness of the apostles, together with five
generations of their successors, to this obvious contingency
of non-orthodox baptism? on what plea can you excuse,
even after the dispute had arisen, those quarrels and delays
which left thousands to live and die under the shadow of
possible damnation?' You may answer: 'God forbid that
we should be driven up against so mechanical a view of
Christ's teaching, or of the operation of the Holy Ghost,
as this!' But that mechanical view is precisely of your
own making. The one liberating word, and the word which
has been all along on the lips of your opponents, is that
which the traditionalist has tried to silence with his theory
of apostolic succession—the one obvious suggestion that
Christ left these questions to natural historical development. The clearer you suppose that compelling mandate
to have been which Christ gave to his church, and the
greater the church's divine right of binding and loosing
Christian consciences, the more hopelessly do you emphasize the fact that the church worked in this case, to
thousands of people, not so much for salvation as for
damnation. It is true, the more liberal view of baptism
finally prevailed, and the western church held that this
sacrament is independent, in theory, of the Christian

ministry or even of Christian status; a heathen can validly
baptize a heathen child, so long as he only performs a
simple act and says a few simple words with the intention
of making a Christian of him[35]. But the point is, that the
opposite view was widespread and long lived. And, if a
priest teaches us now that we, and the thousands with us,
have no right to take St Augustine and St Gregory as
meaning what they said about miracles, then we must
answer that he, or even his superiors, may perhaps prove
as hopelessly mistaken as either St Cyprian or St Augustine
certainly was in this vital matter of heretical baptism.
Any consistent attempt to follow the contrary theory
either violates historical fact or leads, as we have seen, to
painful conclusions which will be most emphatically repudiated by those who in logic are most directly responsible for them. In this baptismal dispute, the traditionalist, like ourselves, is finally compelled to discover the
real operation of the Holy Ghost in a God-directed conflict
of the human mind between two uncertainties, and in the
final victory of the less uncharitable view, with all the more
life in it because it had not been so much imposed by a
legislator without as evolved from conscience within.
Moreover, this baptismal instance is only one of a dozen
such cases. When the question of heretical baptism had
been fairly well settled, it still remained to fight out
whether heretical priestly orders were valid; whether a
heretic could consecrate bread into Christ's body at the
eucharist; and so on. The question of orders cannot be
said to be settled even yet. The papal commission on
Anglican orders, after basing its denial of their validity
upon the absence of formalities which (it was then conclusively proved) had often been omitted even at Roman
ordinations, fell back at last upon the safer ground of
'intention.' There was no proper 'intention' in Anglican
ordinations; and therefore they were not valid. It is
scarcely necessary to point out that, since no mortal being

can ever be absolutely certain of his fellow-mortal's intentions, this theory is as safe from disproof as it is from
proof; and the papal pronouncement against Anglican
orders can hardly be said to have settled the question,
even to a thinking Roman catholic. Long ago, again, the
great Pope Gregory VII pronounced on the sacramental
ministrations of immoral or simoniacal clergy in a sense
which was deliberately reversed by the policy of his successors in the later medieval church, and which, without
being directly contrary to modern orthodoxy, is scarcely
reconcilable with any efficacious theory of divine apostolical guidance[36]. But I must not labour these points,
which I have so far emphasized only because they suggest
obvious questions of which even Mr Turner seems curiously
unconscious.

Let me pause here to avoid a natural misconception.
I have spoken very strongly of certain rigid tenets, which
to thousands of people seem neither true nor edifying,
with regard to those three words *church, ministry* and
*succession*. I say advisedly to thousands, and to educated
thousands who sincerely respect the church and the priest.
We sit in silence Sunday after Sunday, while the priest
often preaches in Christ's name doctrines which to us seem
essentially those which Christ came to sweep away 1900
years ago. We listen in silence, and can only watch the
crucifix over the pulpit and wonder what Christ would say
to these things if he appeared on earth again. It seems to
thousands of us—and the Report of the Archbishops' Committee shows at least a dim appreciation of this fact—that
we are condemned to hear Pharisaism preached in the name
of privileged and exclusive Christianity. These doctrines,
we are convinced, are the traditions of men; doctrines
which cannot even be defined to any practical purpose
without violating the facts of history. And, so believing,
we are so bound to speak; measuring our words indeed,
but not trimming them to expediency or to hollow com-

promise. If the chaplains back from the front describe the
average man's feelings towards the church with a frank
surprise which seems to us somewhat naïve, this is to a
great extent the layman's fault also. So long as we remain
silent, or so long as the only public criticism of the clergy
is made in a carping spirit, so long must misunderstandings
be necessarily numerous, and possibly fatal. The chaplains
recognize clearly and generously that the man in the
trenches is often pathetically anxious to draw nearer to
the church, and that it is the church herself which often
repels him, far more through misunderstanding than
through negligence or deliberate want of charity[37]. But
they seem scarcely to realize, even yet, that what they
now hear in the camp is what they might have heard in.
the market-place any time these thirty years at least; that
even the best-intentioned laity are increasingly unwilling
to take the clergy as their guides; that it is increasingly
rare for men of really liberal education to take holy orders;
and that it is suicidal to attempt to restore the waning
influence of the church by laying more and more stress
upon a doctrine so emphatically repudiated by many historians as that of apostolical succession, and so vaguely
supported even by a scholar of Mr Turner's learning and
enthusiasm. I say advisedly again, *more and more stress*;
for the clerical watchword is now everywhere 'we are
letting the children go; we must teach in the village school,
and in our public secondary schools, such definite church
doctrine as can never be forgotten or obliterated in
maturer age.' This comes perilously near to saying 'let us
teach the boys that which grown men are increasingly unable to believe.' Let all who will hold these doctrines of
church and ministry and succession, so long as they place
them on no false basis, and claim no false sanction for
them. A man's conception of the church is, as most of us
probably hold, mainly a matter of conscience between him
and his God. Therefore, while sympathizing with every

pious opinion on this subject so long as it claims to be no
more than a pious opinion, we hold it fatally mistaken in
any case, and even sinful when it is open-eyed and deliberate, to teach our children highly debatable doctrines
as if they were fundamental certainties[38].

So far every man has a right to protest, and is even
bound to protest, who has gone just enough into this
question to convince himself that the historical evidence
cannot warrant anything like certain affirmation in favour
of the catholic doctrine—to put it in the mildest possible
terms. But this protest must not be misunderstood. These
catchwords are not the only things, by a long way, that we
hear either from the pulpit or from the clergyman outside
the church. The church is—or better still, the churches
are—the greatest organization for good that was ever built
up by the voluntary efforts of mankind. I hope to recur
to this on a later occasion, and to show that the refusal
of obedience to a medieval conception of the church does
not involve religious anarchy, or exclude the deepest respect for all respectable tradition. There is a sense in
which all reasonable people would admit the duty of
listening to the voice of the church; that is, of lending a
sympathetic ear to all teaching that is hallowed by noble
names in the past, and of rejecting nothing in the spirit of
mere wilfulness or levity. But this, which a quaker like
Dr Hodgkin would have admitted, is far removed from
the claims of those who speak to us as if the church were
as definite an organism, with as clear a voice, as the state.
It is those claims, most passionately urged by those who
take least pains to justify them from history, which seem
to stand hopelessly in the way of Christian unity. There
has been general assent to the darker side of the Archbishops' Report; but there is probably equally general
agreement with the chaplains' impression that the average
man would welcome all that is truest in the church, if we
could all start afresh with a hearty desire to find the most

that we can in Christ's personality and teaching, and to tolerate those who there find either less or more than we ourselves do.

In my next lecture, I hope to give a brief sketch of early Franciscan history in illustration of the points emphasized this evening.

# V

THE Roman and Anglo-catholic doctrine of *church, ministry* and *succession* is sometimes supported by an ingenious analogy. It is admitted that the early documents are painfully scanty and obscure. But, after a few generations, we get a clear sight of the Catholic church (that is, of a strong majority of professing Christians), bound together in a fairly definite organization and moving in a fairly definite direction; which direction, on the whole, was fairly consistently maintained until the Reformation. Therefore the upholders of the catholic theory argue: 'If we see a train emerging from a tunnel in a certain direction, and keeping that direction pretty consistently, at any rate until a revolutionary change occurs, then we may infer with some certainty that the train's unseen course through the tunnel was consistent with its visible course followed in the open air.' To those familiar with Alpine railways, the argument will scarcely carry complete conviction even as applied literally to a railway train. As applied to ancient and medieval history, most scholars would probably condemn it, even *a priori*, as involving anachronistic ideas; that regularity which seems normal to the modern man is really rather exceptional in the past, even under the Roman Empire. But we are not left to *a priori* judgment; for we have here a very clear analogy in actual religious history, in the one movement which, by common consent, resembles most nearly the ferment of the apostolic age. If we could destroy all Franciscan documents written within twenty years of the Founder's death, and thin down the rest to the same rarity as early Christian documents, and then attempt to infer the Founder's intentions mainly from the actual direction in which we find the order moving steadily and consistently at the end of its

first century, we should misread some of the most important and most instructive facts in all religious history.
We should then find in actual existence a clerical order,
living mainly by mass-fees and mendicancy; whereas St
Francis had contemplated the priest as exceptional, and
begging only as secondary to handiwork. St Francis,
again, distrusted and discouraged book-learning for his
disciples; yet, long before the century was out, the Franciscans had captured the universities and were causing
widespread scandal by their quarrels for precedence there.
St Francis had said: 'our poor and narrow churches will
preach better even than our words'; but presently the
friars' churches far out-did the average· parish church
both in size and in magnificence; the costliest and richest
of all was built over the saint's own bones, by his own
official successor; and one of St Francis's dearest disciples
lost his life for protesting against this violation of the rule.

For, in St Francis's case, we do get a definite rule laid
down in writing by the Founder, not clear enough to re-
move all doubt on all important points, but quite unambiguous, and phrased with quite legal exactness, on the
most important point of all, the vow of poverty. Here, at
first sight, is a contrast to Christian origins; but in fact
this is only a minor variation which renders the general
resemblance more striking. This existing rule—or these
rules if you will, for there were two editions of it—this
rule came only late in the saint's religious career, which
lasted from about 1207 to 1226. There had been an earlier
rule in 1209 or 1210; but this was simply a collection of
gospel precepts hinging on those verses of St Matthew
which had played so great a part in the Founder's own
conversion: 'As ye go, preach...freely ye have received,
freely give. Provide neither gold nor silver nor brass in
your purses, nor scrip for your journey,' etc.[39]

We get this result, therefore; St Francis's ministry had
already lasted longer than our Lord's brief teaching career

c.                                                                    6 before there was any thought of a rule at all; and that rule, when it came, was simply the gospel rule, no more systematic or detailed than those admittedly fragmentary sayings of Christ which the Evangelists have transmitted to us. More than ten years elapsed before the first really formal rule was drawn up (1221); and by this time St Francis's mission had come far more definitely under the influence of the official church, and the saint used the help of a scholarly disciple, Caesarius of Speyer, in composing his rule. This was entirely rewritten two years later (1223) under still directer influence from the Roman Court. We see, then, that if St Francis's mission had been as brief as Christ's he would have died before it had even occurred to him to secure the movement by formal prescriptions. To be a Franciscan, during the first few years of the mission, was simply to have been converted; to have seen once for all that earthly things are perishable, and only the spirit imperishable; to be ready—in a phrase which Franciscans borrowed now or later from the early Fathers in the Desert, or even from beyond—to be ready to follow, naked, the naked Christ. If, in those days, St Francis had been asked to state a formula of discipleship, he would probably have answered that this would be not only useless but mischievous. Some had given up all to follow him, and were with him by night and day; these men needed no formal certificate of discipleship. But the large majority of those who listened to his teaching must have had wives and children; many of these may have been as devoted as those twelve in whom later Franciscan legend saw a parallel to Christ's twelve apostles; but they had their worldly duties as well as their spiritual calling. Hundreds more must have been in suspense of mind—smoking flax which would have been promptly quenched by any formal rules of profession. St Francis was not concerned to make a body of Franciscans, but to bring men in general to see God and Nature as he saw them. The renunciation of the

world had brought him unspeakable joy and liberty of
spirit; he was only concerned, therefore, to spread the good
tidings that all who will may have the best things in God's
universe even during the present life, and still more in the
next, without money and without price.

But, by inevitable natural growth, this embryo began
to acquire the consistency of a living body. No such body
could grow to maturity within the Roman church without
formal permission from the hierarchy and formal pledges
of obedience. After two years, therefore, St Francis's first
rule was written and, not without much hesitation,
approved verbally by a broad-minded pope, Innocent III.

Here, if the Franciscan documents had left us in the
same dim twilight as that twilight of Christian origins, we
might jump to the conclusion that St Francis's rule of
1210 was of the same pattern as the rules of the other
religious orders. The lover of hard-and-fast formulas
would very naturally say: 'We can safely infer that this
lost religious rule essentially resembled all the others which
have survived, and which resemble each other so closely;
our theory stands firmly on this analogy.' And the rest of
us, while seeing here a very slender foundation for a hard-
and-fast theory of orthodoxy which, by its very nature,
drives many thousands into the limbo of unorthodoxy,
would yet have admitted that the analogy carried with it
a certain amount of presumptive probability. But in
Franciscan history we are not at the mercy of mere
analogy. Although the rule of 1210 has perished, we have
just enough evidence to convince all scholars probably,
and certainly all the best-known scholars on either side,
that it differed essentially from (for instance) the Bene-
dictine rule; that indeed, in this sense, it was scarcely a
rule at all. It was not until the little band of disciples had
grown to many thousands—not until it had long since become obvious that the Founder could not keep personal
touch with all his flock—that the first rule in the ordinary

monastic sense was drawn up. But, though this was at last an unquestionably monastic rule, it differed still. in many ways from its predecessors. However, though it was still very strongly scriptural and hortatory in character, it did in parts aim at the exactness of a legal code. The prescriptions as to poverty were precise and severe; they fill a whole octavo page in the rule of 1221, and are summed up in the rule of 1223 by the following sentence: ' I enjoin strictly upon all the brethren that in no wise they receive money or coin, either directly or through a third person '— *per interpositam personam.* This was, as we have seen, formally ratified in a Papal bull.

Therefore, in order to test the 'tunnel' theory, we have only to take a brief glance at the next hundred years of Franciscan history. In this case we can follow the course of the young society very closely through that first crucial century which, in Christian history, has been compared to the dark tunnel. Tracing it thus through the most un-exceptionable documents, mostly official, how much support shall we find for the theory that what the catholic church was confessedly doing in 90 A.D. and what it did fairly consistently for fourteen succeeding centuries, must have been that which the Founder had clearly prescribed? You will find, I think, that the Franciscan facts are directly opposed to that theory.

The rule of 1223 had already modified that of 1221, though very slightly, in the laxer direction. Between this time and the saint's death, we have the testimony of the closest disciples, and even of an official biographer like Celano, that the order had already begun to drift steadily backwards from its original ideal. Reading between the lines, we can see clearly (what might have been anticipated *a priori*) that this reaction was favoured by the official Roman church. St Francis, shortly before his death, had resigned the official direction of the order partly for reasons of health; this, again, naturally hastened the process of

relaxation. A few months before the end, the saint issued
a last and most pathetic appeal. Forgetting his present
official nothingness, he spoke to the order with the authority of one who had originally begotten them all in the
gospel, and passionately adjured them never to relax
their ideal of absolute poverty, nor even to suffer glosses
on the rule. That rule, he pleaded, is absolutely plain and
precise, needing no gloss or explanation: and, that the
saint spoke truly here, nobody will deny who takes the
trouble to read its prescriptions on the subject of poverty.

A few weeks after writing this Testament he died; two
years later he was sainted, and thenceforth the flock
prayed to him as one who looked down upon them from
the presence of God. Yet all this while, the large majority
of them steadily ignored, not only his Last Discourse, his
Testament, but even the plain prescriptions of his rule.
A money-box was set up at Assisi for the great and costly
basilica that was to enshrine his bones. Protests were
raised by the earlier disciples; some of these saved their
life or liberty by fleeing to desert hermitages; but Caesarius
of Speyer, who had helped to compose the rule of 1221, was
cast into prison, and finally knocked on the head by a
rough jailor who suspected him of attempting to escape.
Thus the proto-martyr of Franciscanism, after the saint's
death, was a man who had clung too faithfully to the rule
and the Testament. About the same time, in 1230, the
Testament itself was submitted to the judgment of Pope
Gregory IX, who, as Cardinal Ugolino, had been St Francis's personal friend and the official protector of the order.
Gregory decided clearly and unequivocally that this
Testament, the most passionate of all the Founder's
letters to his brethren, had no binding force. The rule
itself was now so glossed as to allow the order to possess
property and to receive money, providing only that this
should be done under decent cover of a third person. Two
clear threads run along all the rest of our journey

through this historical tunnel. On the one hand, the hierarchy and the majority of Franciscan officials busied themselves with inventing more and more specious methods of raising money without formally acknowledging receipt, and of accumulating lands and houses under a continued profession of naked poverty. On the other hand, they took increasingly severe measures against that minority which still insisted upon actually living the life which all alike had vowed to live. These latter called themselves *Spirituals*, and have been christened from outside by the less sympathetic name of *Zelanti*, or Zealots. They were led by some of the earliest and most intimate of the saint's disciples; their stronghold was in the mountain districts to which he himself had belonged, and in such little hermitages as he himself had loved. Few bodies in all Christian history have a purer record than theirs, until conflict drove them into exaggeration. The story is admirably told in the third volume of Dr H. C. Lea's *History of the Inquisition in the Middle Ages*, and, from a different standpoint, in Mr A. G. Ferrers Howell's *S. Bernardino of Siena*. Mr Howell, who worked through the original documents in entire independence of Lea, comes to strikingly similar conclusions; and I seize this opportunity of recommending to you a very valuable book which has never received the full recognition it deserves. These Spirituals, when it became evident that the majority were bent upon relaxation, would have been only too glad for permission to separate into a distinct order of their own. But neither the hierarchy nor the authorities were willing to show the whole world so plainly that St Francis could no longer be literally obeyed within the Franciscan order. The Spirituals, therefore, were still kept in bondage under their persecutors, except where they found it possible to save themselves by flight. A friendly prelate said once to one of them whom for a while he protected: 'Brother Liberato, brother Liberato, I swear unto thee by him who created me, that never has

a poor man's flesh been sold so dearly as I might have sold
thine; thy brethren would drink thy very blood, if they
could[40].' Many of them were driven into rebellion; they
then called themselves 'The little brethren'—*Fraticelli*.
These Fraticelli, like all other outlaws, were soon joined
by a herd of Adullamites; and it is possible that the
accusations of immorality made against them by the
orthodox of later times have some real foundation in fact.
But many, in spite of all persecution, remained true to
their Founder both in the letter and in the spirit. There
are few darker religious tragedies than the Auto-da-Fé of
Marseilles in 1318. Twenty-five Spirituals had been arrested
by the Inquisition; through threats and the slow torture
of prison, these were weeded down to four, who were
finally burned alive. The formal sentence of condemnation
is extant; it specifies a number of errors, each of which
separately was judged to be heretical and worthy of the
death-penalty. One of these was that they refused to beg
for corn and oil and wine to be laid up in the convent
stores; a point on which St Francis would unquestionably
have taken their side without a moment's hesitation[41].
Indeed, they were justified here even by the formal decision of a pope and a general council; but that pope was
dead and gone; the present pope, the live pope, was he
whose contrary decree had changed his predecessor's pronouncement into a new heresy. This is what documentary
history discloses within what may be called the tunnel-
century of Franciscanism.

The story of the variations within the order in the
matter of book-learning is even more instructive in one
way, because it affords us an exact parallel to this modern
plea that the character and direction of St Ignatius's
church, when it emerges into clear historical light about
90 A.D., must necessarily have been the character and
direction of Christ's personal disciples two generations
earlier. One of the most learned scholars in this field is a

Swiss Franciscan, Father Hilarius Felder, who has written a valuable and very exhaustive book on *Franciscanism and Learning during the First Half of the 13th Century*. The book bears a remarkable family resemblance to these laborious apologetic essays which have appeared under Professor Swete's auspices. Just as the general tenor of Christ's teaching, and his attitude towards formalities of every kind, create a general presumption against his having prescribed, or even sympathized with, any precise and elaborate organization—just as some of his actual recorded words seem almost to exclude such an idea—so not only is St Francis explicitly recorded to have discouraged book-learning, but it is difficult to conceive how his disciples could possibly have studied, at a time when they might not call anything their own, and when the saint himself, having once heard them speak of his wretched little hut as 'Francis's cell,' steadfastly refused ever to use it again[42]. Therefore the modern apologist's task in both cases is similar; Father Felder on the one hand, the essayists on the other, have to present the early evidence in a light as far removed as possible from these unfavourable, though strictly historical, presumptions. Moreover, this task is in both cases facilitated by the scantiness and obscurity of the documentary evidence; for Franciscan documents do not here give us those exact stages and those precise dates by which we can trace the money question so clearly. The essayists reach firm ground from their point of view, as we have seen, at the end of about two generations—about 90 A.D.—and have henceforward little difficulty in proving the existence and spread of catholic ideas. Father Felder, in a field that is naturally richer in documents, reaches his goal with the generalate of St Bonaventura, only one generation after the Founder's death. St Bonaventura was a learned man, Professor of Theology at Paris, the greatest university in the world; therefore we should scarcely wonder (even if we did not

know independently how far the order had already
drifted away from strict poverty) to find in St Bonaventura
a stout champion of book-learning. Roger Bacon, his
almost exact contemporary, speaks of his own fellow-
Franciscans and the Dominicans as 'the student orders[43].'
The Friars had indeed become the learned orders within a
short time of St Francis's death; they, who might originally possess nothing, were now growing rich in books.
These men, to whom their Founder had expressly repeated
Christ's prohibition 'be ye not called Master,' were fighting
at the universities, to the detriment of their popularity
and spiritual ascendancy both inside and outside, for the
Master's degree and its attendant privileges. St Bonaventura did most certainly encourage and systematize
learning within the order; and popes did the same; a bull
of 1279 evidently contemplates Franciscan libraries of
considerable size. Father Felder, therefore, instinctively
takes the year 1260 and the generalate of Bonaventura as
his real starting-point in argument, just as the essayists
virtually start with the end of the first Christian century,
arguing backwards from the state of things they find then
existing. But you will see that, in Franciscan history, we
have very strong evidence even in the matter of book-
learning, and the clearest official evidence in the more
vital matter of money, to prove that this adventurous
process of reasoning would lead us very far away from the
truth. Much of this danger, as I have said before, seems
to be recognized by the essayists themselves; their vagueness at crucial points can scarcely be other than the deliberate and intentional reserve of men too learned and too
candid to dogmatize where dogma is felt to be out of place.
Yet this reserve has its ambiguous side, and leaves room
for very mischievous dogmatism in other less responsible
quarters. *The Church Times*, not content with a long review
of the book, publishes also a leading article which concludes: 'Mr Turner and his fellow workers present a far

stronger case for certain traditions of the church than has ever been known before[44]'; and *The Church Times* is, of course, the steady champion of dogmatic views on these subjects. The bishop of Oxford, four years ago, had already claimed Mr Turner among those historians who have strengthened 'the distinctive Catholic position about the Apostolic succession of the ministry and the place of the Episcopate[45].' Those ambiguities, therefore, of which Canon Wilson complained at Cambridge as presenting a serious hindrance to spiritual life, have not been removed by these recent attempts to meet his clear challenge. Would it not have been in the interests of the church—which, by universal consent, is on her trial in this furnace of war and social unrest—to confess quite plainly and unambiguously that the current catholic conceptions of church, ministry, and succession are pious opinions, historically unprovable, and rejected by many historians?—most people, I think, would go further, and say, by a considerable majority of historians. Of course a pious opinion, however unpopular, may possibly, in the long run, prove true in spite of all historians; for it can at least be pleaded in favour of historical scholars that they have never yet laid formal claim to individual or collective infallibility. But it never can be right to pass off a pious opinion as an historical fact until it has won the suffrages of at least the generality of historical students; and that would seem to be a fatal policy of reserve which permits the extremists of *The Church Times* to draw encouragement for their own dogmatic views from the diplomatic hesitancy of Professor Swete's collaborators. A pious opinion which by its very nature and essence unchurches thousands of Christians, and which also dresses itself in false colours to command their obedience, approaches perilously near to impiety. Any catholic has a personal and individual right to believe in these exclusive doctrines; but none has the right to force upon the public, as a law of God, that which is only matter

of individual taste, or which at most expresses only the
consensus of a certain number of individual preferences.
To put pious opinions in their right place is not destruction
but construction.

For it must be noted that these particular opinions, in
those cruder forms which present such an obstacle to
Christian union, are not even catholic in the truest sense.
A far broader view, perfectly consistent with modern
historical research, is implicit in perhaps the greatest
catholic of the last generation, Cardinal Newman, and has
been clearly expressed by one of the most learned products of modern catholicism, Abbé Loisy. Loisy, it is true,
has been unchurched by his co-religionists, and left to
protest (in Father Tyrrell's words) that he might be cut
off from the consecrated communion bread at Easter;
but not from the unleavened bread of sincerity and truth[46].
Loisy, however, was condemned for facing unflinchingly
the conclusions logically implied in Newman, whose
attempts to reconcile faith with history brought upon him
the dislike and suspicion of all meaner minds within his
own communion. Darwinism—the doctrine of evolution
—hailed at first as Antichrist, has already been assimilated
more or less by nearly all Christians; it is a commonplace
now to explain Christian development by references to
development in animal and vegetable life. But, before
Darwin wrote, Newman had already written his own essay
on Development in Religion, even as, a century earlier
still, the German protestant Lessing had applied the same
principles in that essay on the Education of the Human
Race, which was translated into English a generation ago
by F. W. Robertson of Brighton. It may almost be said
that the idea of development had been grasped earlier by
religious thinkers than by natural philosophers; for it is
implicit in St Augustine's *City of God*, and one of the
earliest theories of the kind was thought out by the blessed
Joachim of Fiore, who died when St Francis was a boy.

Even St Ignatius, about 90 A.D., probably recognized a
considerable process of development between the apostles
and himself, just as all historians admit a long development
since St Ignatius. But Newman carried the idea farther
than anybody else. Perceiving clearly how widely the
modern catholics differed from their apostolic predecessors,
he sought a philosophic justification for this process of
change. Loisy, in our own day, has only pushed Newman's
ideas to their logical conclusions, first independently and
then with conscious reference to his predecessor. Those
conclusions may be best understood by a sentence or two
from Mr W. J. Williams's book, *Pascal, Newman and Loisy*;
though all who can should read Loisy's own *L'Evangile et
l'Eglise*, a book of such brilliant transparency as we find
only in the best French writing, very brief, but now run up
to five times its original price because it was forbidden by
the hierarchy after it had passed through two editions.
Mr Williams writes on p. 299: 'Christ spoke of a Kingdom
of Heaven, a Kingdom of God in which He was to reign—
a Kingdom which was to come in the clouds of Heaven
apparently within the lifetime of those whom he addressed.
As that great critic and historian the Abbé Loisy has
shown, it is not necessary for the catholic apologist, and
it is impossible for the historian and critic, to suppose that
Christ clearly and fully foresaw what would take place....
This would be heresy if pressed and fully described, for it
would assume that Christ had not a really human soul or
human mind, but something phantasmic, not dependent
upon the senses in the ordinary way or needing the labour
and diligence of a man. If Christ had not the trials and
difficulties of mental learning, obscurity and toil, as well
as physical hunger and weariness, He would cease to be
altogether our example or to suffer from some of the most
peculiarly human of all our difficulties, and His great
sacrifice, in living and dying for us, His great atonement
of man with God, would be unavailing for the mind, the

soul, the intellect of man. Persons, who have committed themselves to a mechanical conception of the mode in which Christ lived in the Beatific Vision and have thereby caused a sort of annihilation of all the specially human qualities of His soul, are on the verge of a heresy the most completely destructive of the whole Christian idea which it is possible to name.'

You may be startled by this approving summary by a catholic of a catholic's words—both, men who asserted their right to retain their full privileges in the Roman communion, though one has in fact been excommunicated. But we need not be so deeply surprised; all Christians who look first of all towards Christ, and gaze upon him with a single eye, must needs be drawn very close together as time advances, in spite of the efforts of other Christians to separate them. When we are all steering for the same lodestar, our different courses are certain to show more parallelism than divergence. Protestants have learned a great deal from catholics; and catholics are learning here, you will think, from protestants. Abbé Loisy does, as a matter of fact, employ his theory of development as the basis for a very able defence of catholicism against protestantism, to which I have no time to do justice here. He even argues, and Mr Williams with him, that catholicism can better afford than protestantism to face the plain facts of church history. We need not quarrel about that; if indeed the catholic is studying history even more truly and sincerely than we trust we ourselves are, then so much the better for all parties. The real thing here—the real gospel, we may almost call it—is this, that by dint of facing independently the actual facts of history these hitherto irreconcilable adversaries are drawing astonishingly near to each other, both in truth and in charity. This question is well illustrated not only by the Franciscan analogy but also by the celebrated controversy between Bossuet and Leibnitz—a controversy memorable for the

fame of its protagonists, who were among the great figures
of all history, and perhaps still more exceptional in their
mutual forbearance, their avoidance of petty issues, and
the sincere desire of both parties for the reunion of
Christendom. Of that, however, there could be no hope
after Bossuet had plainly declared that he could not for a
moment entertain any suggestion of going back upon the
decrees of the Council of Trent; that he was always ready
to *explain* those decrees to an honest doubter, but could
never treat them as *questionable*. Bossuet, as an orthodox
Roman catholic, had no other answer possible; Leibnitz,
as an historian who knew very well how far the Council of
Trent had advanced beyond the claims even of medieval
catholicism, could not possibly accept those terms of un-
conditional submission[47]. But there was one capital point
upon which Leibnitz reduced even Bossuet to silence[48].
He showed conclusively that the Council of Trent, in de-
creeing the canonicity of those books which protestants
separate as apocryphal from the strict canon of the Bible,
had contradicted the general consensus of the whole church
for fifteen centuries. 'If ever any catholic doctrine has
been taught "always and everywhere," it is that doctrine
of the Old Testament canon which the protestants hold[49].'
So concludes Leibnitz, and Bossuet has no valid historical
evidence to oppose to him. Moreover, Leibnitz exposes
very clearly the flimsy foundations upon which his
opponent had until then based his defence[50]. The early
fathers constantly used the phrases 'sacred scriptures' or
'divine books' with the most extraordinary laxity, apply-
ing them not only to the so-called Apocrypha, but even to
such books as the *Epistles* of St Clement and the *Shepherd*
of Hermas, which the church has never seriously counted
as canonical. In this laxer sense, the Old Testament
Apocrypha is often spoken of as 'divine.' On the other
hand, when early or medieval scholars undertook to
enumerate the canonical books in the strictest sense, these

lists correspond on the whole to the protestant enumera-
tion, and very seldom justify that of the fathers of
Trent. In short, the Tridentine theory depends largely,
even for such show of truth as can be urged for it, upon
that habitual laxity of definition which is one of the main
difficulties in early church history[51]. We have here a close
analogy to the triple problem of church, ministry, and
succession. The one thing which emerges clearly from the
essays in Dr Swete's volume is the extreme vagueness of
the early evidence, and the frequent employment of the
most important words in very different senses. Early
fathers were habitually as indefinite as Bossuet himself
was, on occasion, about different conceptions of the church;
they thought vaguely, and these mental ambiguities
blurred their language. We cannot import into history a
distinctness which never existed in actual minds or among
actual events of the past, and which was never even aimed
at until that ancient world had disappeared to make room
for the modern. The fathers of Trent blundered more
obviously, but not, I think, more fundamentally, than
those who try to read modern clearness of definition back
into the first Christian century. If this could be more
generally recognized, the different Christian bodies would
already be far nearer to each other. Many of us may
infinitely prefer the books of Wisdom or Ecclesiasticus,
though the early church places them in the second rank,
to Esther which she places in the first. We may, in fact,
agree so far here with the Roman catholic judgment; we
must only beware of standing upon the false historical
ground which that judgment implies. So also we may
infinitely prefer episcopacy to presbyterianism, the idea
of apostolic succession to the idea of a free and indis-
criminate ministry; but a vast step will have been taken
if we accept these preferences for what they are worth, and
admit that history gives us no certain ground for them.
And this admission may, in itself, change for ever our

sense of values. We shall then ask ourselves seriously what weight a personal prepossession deserves, when weighed in the scale against our chances of reaching unity with others whose prepossessions are different.

If truth says (with him who said *I am the truth*): 'I bring you not peace, but a sword' yet she says also: 'My peace I leave with you: not as the world giveth, give I unto you.' Christian charity can only be based upon Christian truth. At first sight, would not all unbiassed thinkers be loth to accept a Christian theory which deliberately keeps millions of fellow-Christians at arm's length, and which, in cases where one of our party fraternizes too much with an opposing party, would cut him off from religious communion with the majority? And, so long as this exclusivist theory remains admittedly unproven within the realm of history, are not its supporters morally bound to uphold it only as a pious opinion? and are not their adversaries, when it claims an historical basis, justified in doubting even of its piety? Newman seldom wrote a more significant sentence than that melancholy confession in 1845: 'The chief, perhaps the only English writer who has any claim to be considered an ecclesiastical historian, is the infidel Gibbon*.'· When those who claim to be God's plenipotentiaries refuse to render unto history the things which are history's, are they not doing their best to repel the average man from rendering unto God the things that are God's?

* See note 9 at the end of this book.

# VI

WHERE do we stand, then, if we frankly accept the necessity of a new reformation, based on the recognition that the exclusive spirit in Christianity is falling more and more into open bankruptcy? Exclusiveness is not Christian charity, whatever specious arguments it may find, and with whatever real virtues it may ally itself; for no student of history will deny the real virtues of individuals or churches which have maintained these exclusive doctrines. Man is a strange compound, consistent neither in virtue nor in vice, but living by all sorts of compromises. We must confess of ourselves that we are never likely to live up to our full ideal of good; and fortunately, on the other hand, even a false ideal cannot altogether poison the human mind; the exclusivist theory has its redeeming virtues, or it would never have won its way so far. Even when, as historical students, we are obliged to wage the most implacable war against certain ideas, we must be ready to learn in other ways from their advocates. The pious historians who, for many centuries, have solemnly fed the public with what they knew subconsciously to be more or less false, starting with mere suppressions of inconvenient fact and sometimes ending with something far more definite and deliberate than even the suggestion of falsehood—those pious purveyors of misrepresentation, who can be named by the dozen and are not altogether absent from any party, have often been really religious persons, betrayed into that one bosom-sin by an evil tradition which permits and even prescribes a certain want of scruple in defence of the faith. We see the same in political life. Robespierre, who deluged France with blood, had in earlier life resigned a lucrative and honourable position because it might have compelled him to con-

demn criminals to death. Lenin and Trotzky, before they
came into actual power, were doubtless quite as sincere in
their hatred of the death-penalty as Robespierre. As cold
statistics show, the moral difference between exclusivist
and non-exclusivist in religion is not overwhelming, when
we state it arithmetically. But in religion or in morals there
is no difference that we can treat as absolutely negligible.
When Christ bade us judge men and parties by their
fruits, he anticipated that sentence quoted by William
James from a modern workman's lips: 'There's not much
difference between one man and another; but it's just that
little difference that counts.' Let me quote two concrete
cases which I have lately met with in two parishes where
the priests were unusually efficient, sincere, and charitable
high-churchmen. In each case, a presbyterian came into
the parish, and desired to come to the communion table,
while the priest felt conscientiously bound to repel him.
In each case, the priest applied to the bishop to learn
whether there was no escape from this invidious action;
the bishop answered, no doubt quite truly, that anglican
law and discipline were perfectly clear on this point. The
painful impression created by these incidents even among
anglicans was only heightened by the personal respect
felt for the actors on both sides. Zeller has pointed out
that the case of Galileo would not have been half so
significant, but for the personal character of the chief
actors there. The pope was not at all anxious, personally,
to burn the philosopher; and Galileo, of all philosophers,
would least have enjoyed the honours of the stake. It was
not two men, but two systems that were in irreconcilable
conflict; free science and an exclusive church. If exclusivism be indeed an error, as very large numbers of people
believe, then our personal respect for those who hold it
should only strengthen our resolve to break the barriers
down. We do not spare a disease because we respect the
patient. If all those who try to follow Christ, or wish to

try, are ever to meet together in any sort of brotherhood after this war, then the catholic must at least be ready to consider seriously whether he does Christ service by denying the name of Christian to any man who would rather choose Christ for his master than another; or, again, by repelling those who would gladly kneel with him in that commemoration of which Christ said to his followers: 'This do in remembrance of me[52].'

The new reformation—let us not be afraid of this word—must stand on the broadest and most inclusive basis. This, of course, will involve the greatest possible liberty for divergent conceptions of the ministry and of apostolic succession. Here, again, it must compel the exclusivist to ask himself, 'Am I really following New Testament precedent?'

For there is one biblical case in which the exclusive idea of succession would seem to break down hopelessly. The apostle *par excellence*, the man to whom ancient and medieval theologians refer habitually as '*the* apostle,' owed nothing officially to his brother apostles. His office came straight from Christ, by a mystical consecration to Christ's work. We have the assertion of his independence under his own hand, in the Epistle to the Galatians; he goes even further when necessary, and speaks with some contempt of those who 'seemed to be somewhat' and would have bound him in the shackles of their own exclusivism; he tells us frankly how he withstood Peter to his face when Peter denied the right of the uncircumcised to share in the Christian gospel. Peter had on his side the argument of the modern bishop, who will tell us that the complainant has the remedy in his own hands. Let the presbyterian be confirmed, and he may come and kneel beside us without any breach of Christian charity; let the gentile get himself circumcised, and the problem is solved! But Paul's position was, that we have no right thus to purchase unity at the expense of Christian liberty, except in small cases

where charity bids us defer to the scruples of weaker
brethren; and I need scarcely remind you that priests
and bishops, when they exclude presbyterians, do not
regard themselves as weaker brethren pleading *in forma
pauperis* at the bar of those who stand on stronger Christian ground. There is a strong movement now for Life and
Liberty (to quote its official title) within the Anglican
church. Many of you, I hope, were at that meeting about
a year ago which was addressed on this subject at Cambridge by one of the most respected of living Anglicans.
The speaker said he would go to the root of the matter,
and indeed he spoke very freely more than once. He described, with many touches of that perfectly effective
satire which is possible only to intense moral conviction,
the political delays and even the political shifts and tricks
which, under the present establishment, are necessary
before a new bishopric can be founded even where it is
most urgently needed; meanwhile, of course, the hungry
sheep look up and are not fed. 'This,' he concluded, 'is
what it takes to make a successor to the apostles!' But
did he indeed go here to the promised root of the matter?
Is not the real root this, that George Fox was a truer
successor to the apostles than half the bishops of his day,
protestant or catholic or orthodox of the Greek church?
Does it not ever occur to the catholic that, if any man
arose to-morrow and claimed to have revived in his own
person St Paul's experience of direct conversion and direct
commission from Christ, the church herself would have no
means of testing him but that simple criterion by which
Fox would certainly rise superior to the average seventeenth
century bishop: 'By their fruits ye shall know them[53]?'
It is startling; but can we, on calm reflection, decide otherwise? This new man, we are assuming, makes exactly
St Paul's claims of a vision, a direct message, and direct
inspiration not through flesh and blood. The purely historical evidence might be even stronger in his case than in

St Paul's, whose own authentic account of the conversion events is not easily reconcilable on all points with St Luke's account, so that the book of the Acts brings us almost as much embarrassment as corroboration. What convinced St Paul's brother-apostles was, in the last resort, not his own *ex parte* assertions, not the testimony of his travelling-companions, who might have been biased or hypnotized, but the visible operation of the spirit of Christ within him. A Paul who had never risen any higher above his fellows than to repel them successfully from the Lord's Supper would never have fought his way to the recognition of his divine mandate. We all know that the true seal of the saint's apostleship was in his conversion of the gentiles,— sorely, at first, against the will of his senior, orthodox, and more apostolically regular colleagues. In the last resort, what other test of his mission was there then, or what is there now?

To this the catholic may answer with scornful superiority: 'Show me a St Paul to-day, a real St Paul, and I will acknowledge him!' But it will be seen that our argument does not depend upon the production of an actual Paul at any given moment; it is only necessary to assume the bare possibility of the existence of such a Paul sooner or later, in present or future history. If the catholic admits that one such might possibly arise, with authority straight from Christ to rebuke those that 'seem to be somewhat' in the church, and to break down the most time-honoured barriers of separation, then this one possible and hypothetical exception, if there were no more, would seem fatal to the strict succession theory. And no thinking catholic would dare to deny this possibility: the pope in council would never dare to deny it. For we should then have the spectacle of men speaking, in the name of the Holy Ghost, words of solemn dishonour against the Holy Ghost. Those who most definitely claim to guard the deposit of belief in the Holy Spirit's absolute divinity and omnipotence, would be found denying God's power to raise up a second Paul. Can we hope for any full 'life and liberty' until all Christians have first recognized the possibility that Christ may have given no clearer rule of apostolic succession than that criterion by which even popes would be obliged ultimately to judge: 'By their fruits ye shall know them'?

In reasoning thus with our opponents, however, we must beware of showing ourselves unreasonable, if only by an exaggeration of essential truths. While pressing them to face the logical consequences of their own theories, we may legitimately wonder in our own minds how they have failed to grasp considerations which to us seem so self-evident, and why they have needed a world-war to make them realize that some such thoughts as these have been fermenting, for thirty years at least, in the minds of those who sit in silence under their sermons. But we must not allow this personal wonder to affect our argument, nor to tempt us into any *a priori* assumption that these differences of opinion between us and them do actually arise from their blindness rather than from our own. Though there are some obvious difficulties which they seem to shirk, they emphasize other considerations which cannot lightly be dismissed. I think, however, that, if you analyze carefully the different pleas urged against such concessions as I have advocated, you will find they all fall under four headings. We are told either (1) 'what you urge is fundamentally false,' or (2) 'the liberty you claim is morally dangerous,' or (3) 'you would find it very cold and uncomfortable,' or (4) (the exact opposite of this): 'men choose the course you advocate in order to shirk the real difficulties of Christianity.' Let me take these objections in order.

(1) The first, and perhaps the most frequent of all, we need not seriously answer, for it is sheer dogmatism. If a pastor takes it as axiomatic that he cannot condescend to

meet his flock on the common ground of reason, and if he
stigmatizes any such proposal as fundamentally wrong, he
has only himself to thank when he finds himself losing
their hearts.

(2) But it is infinitely dangerous, we are told, to cast
away the safeguards of church and ministry and succession;
such liberty will degenerate into license; there is safety
only within the traditional fold. Fifty years ago, this was
a far stronger argument; for then the fold was still comparatively tranquil, and those who went out found few
like-minded companions. To many minds, the argument
must still appeal very strongly; for in religion, as in every
other department of life, successful association is a real
test of progress; majorities, though not infallible, are very
important factors in civilization. But I ask you to consider very earnestly whether you believe in your own
hearts either that the religious state of those who still
acquiesce in the exclusivist theory is so satisfactory, or
that the quantity and quality of those who are drifting
into more or less acknowledged nonconformity is so in-
considerable, as to make acquiescence the morally safer
course in these days of ours. Some risk we must necessarily
take; no man ever snatched success but from amid risks;
birth was a risk, life is a risk; only the corpse risks nothing,
or the living man so far as he can manage to bury his talent
in a napkin. Christ and his apostles took the moral risk of
association with publicans and sinners; Christ, in teaching
the Samaritan woman that the worship of the future should
not be bound to holy places, but should be in spirit and in
truth, took the risk of encouraging self-conceit and ego-
tistical particularism in religion. St Paul so preached the
doctrine of God's glory manifested in forgiveness of sins
through grace, as to provoke the retort: 'What shall we
say then? Shall we continue in sin, that grace may
abound?' That objection is more difficult to meet in strict
logic, perhaps, than any other argument emphasizing the

easy passage from liberty to license; strictly, the Pauline doctrine of grace would seem to afford a logical justification to antinomianism. But the apostle answers with a cry of the heart—'God forbid! We that are dead to sin, how shall we continue any longer therein?' The man who welcomes God's grace, just because he believes in it with head and heart, is the last man in the world to take God's grace for a license to sin. In the case of those who might catch at the husk of the doctrine of grace simply as an excuse for moral laxity, we are perhaps as helpless as the Anglo-catholic is with those who make confession and absolution a similar excuse for immorality, or the Roman catholic with those thousands who, at least from the thirteenth century onwards, chose to believe that they could buy from the pardon-monger a pennyworth or two-pennyworth of indulgence for sin; for this complaint comes not only from Wyclif and Luther, but from the most orthodox and unexceptionable witnesses also[54]. If we are sure of the honesty of our own choice, then it is not faith, but superstition, which tempts us to lay more stress on the evil that might be than on the good that shall be, so surely as we trust in it and fix our gaze upon it. What is superstition? asked one of the greatest of Cambridge scholars of the seventeenth century, John Smith the Platonist—'An over-timorous and dreadful apprehension of the Deity.... And therefore the true cause and rise of superstition is indeed nothing else but a false opinion of the Deity, that renders him dreadful and terrible, as being rigorous and imperious; that which represents him as austere and fit to be angry, but yet impotent, and easy to be appeased again by some flattering devotions, especially if performed with sanctimonious shows, and a solemn sadness of mind[55].' Let us entertain no such fears, but let us rather trust that, choosing the narrow path, we shall most certainly find Christ walking there at our side. 'John Baptist' (writes St Gregory) 'died not in the direct confession of Christ, but

for telling the truth in a matter of righteousness; yet, seeing
that Christ is truth, therefore in dying for truth he died for
Christ[56].' If, therefore, we have indeed chosen the narrow
path, then, whether seen or unseen, Christ walks there with
us; the direction itself being true, it must follow that every
minute brings us so much nearer to the goal. Doubts there
will necessarily be; for, here again, all life is doubt; but we
may possess our souls in a patience as steadfast as any
other man's, and echo Newman's 'one step enough for me'
without for one moment accepting his general direction[57].

For here, in Newman's case, we may find one of the
strangest ironies of religious history. The spectre that
haunted him all his life was not low church, but broad
church. Arnold of Rugby and other contemporaries
seemed to him to be emptying the Bible of all inspiration,
and Christ of all divinity. One of the things that emerge
most clearly from Newman's wonderful autobiography is
this, that at first, and for many years, he feared Rome only
one degree less than infidelity, and that it was the spectre
of rationalism always stalking behind which drove him
most reluctantly into the Roman church[58]. Once there,
he was too honest to shut his eyes to the fact, which he
had seen clearly all through, that there was an enormous
gulf between papal Rome of 1845 A.D. and apostolic
Jerusalem of 45 A.D. This gulf he bridged by his theory of
development. But a bridge, once made, can be crossed in
either direction. Less than a generation after Newman's
death, Loisy, one of the most distinguished scholars in the
Roman church, convinced himself from the closest study
of the documents that we must deny biblical inspiration,
in the old mechanical sense, far more emphatically than
Arnold denied it; and Loisy's belief in Christ's divinity
became far less definite than the faith of those 'infidels'
whose multiplication had driven Newman Romewards.
But Loisy's theory of development, which in principle was
exactly Newman's theory, enabled him to pass from

orthodox Romanism to this rationalist point of view without breach of logical continuity. The things which repelled Newman from us, and which drove him in abhorrence to Rome, are precisely those principles and facts which, according to Loisy, a Romanist may accept in even more liberal forms than an Anglican. This example, if there were no more, may show how truly the kingdom of god is within us. There is no citadel of safe acquiescence in this world; the bark of St Peter itself is not built in water-tight compartments; 'experience, like a sea, soaks all-effacing in.' The venture of spiritual liberty is the real venture of faith. Those who dare not go forth and try to meet the man from the trenches on common ground, have not even the faith of a good pagan like Socrates, who trusted that truth, however austere, would never fail the honest and patient searcher.

When Socrates, standing on the brink of the grave and yet in full bodily and mental vigour—when Socrates, in the last few minutes before his execution as an atheist, discoursed on the immortality of the soul—he had to face the difficulty always felt by human minds which honestly admit uncertainties, and which steel themselves to the possible abandonment of cherished beliefs for the sake of truths greater and more imperishable, though less tangible[59]. 'How melancholy,' he said, 'if there be such a thing as truth or certainty or possibility of knowledge, that a man should have lighted upon some argument or other which at first seemed true and then turned out to be false and, instead of blaming himself and his own want of wit, because he is annoyed, should at last be too glad to transfer the blame from himself to arguments in general, and for ever afterwards should...lose truth and the knowledge of realities....Let us then, in the first place...rather say that *we* have not yet attained to soundness in ourselves, and that we must struggle manfully and do our best to gain health of mind—you and all other men having regard

to the whole of your future life, and I myself in the pro-
spect of death.' And such also was the temper of his disciples. 'I feel myself' (says Simmias in the same dialogue)
'how hard, or rather impossible, is the attainment of any
certainty about questions such as these in the present life.
And yet I should deem him a coward who did not prove
what is said about them to the uttermost, or whose heart
failed him before he had examined them on every side.
For he should persevere until he has achieved one of two
things; either he should discover, or be taught the truth
about them; or, if this be impossible, I would have him
take the best and most irrefragable of human theories,
and let this be the raft upon which he sails through life—
not without risk, as I admit—if he cannot find some word
of God which will more surely and safely carry him.'

Cannot Christians rise to this height? Does loyalty to
our profession ever require that we should turn our faces
away from a single fact, or even from a single considerable
probability? Was it not one of the greatest of Christian
apologists, bishop Butler, who wrote 'things and actions
are what they are, and the consequences of them will be
what they will be; why then should we desire to be deceived[60]?' If Christ did not in fact institute the catholic
church even in that rudimentary form which we find in
St Ignatius—and still less, the church of later medieval
development—why should we wish to be deceived? Or,
even if there is still serious doubt about it—if hundreds of
scholars, studying the documents and traditions, are unable
to find clear historical ground for the theory—why should
we base our creed upon it, teach it as a dogmatic certainty,
or impose it upon the plastic children whose stiffer parents
refuse to accept it? However dear the illusion may be, we
can deceive nobody in the long run but ourselves—if indeed
we ourselves can so be deceived.

(3) If the doctrine of Socrates and bishop Butler seems
austere, this brings us naturally to the third class of ob-

jection. We are told that to venture forth from the fold of acquiescence is a cold and uncomfortable thing for the human soul.

I cannot see that Christ's was altogether a comfortable doctrine, in this sense. From the very first, the objector here lays himself open to what seems an unanswerable retort. In a poem named after Dante's 'Great Refusal' Mr Godfrey Bradby represents one friend pleading the comforting nature of orthodox doctrines to dissuade another from doubt. To this the doubter answers:

'Yes but, supposing, (since in things divine
Contentment may not be the Pearl of Price),
Yours was the Great Refusal, friend, and mine
The Sacrifice[61]?'

Christ, like Socrates, was not afraid of repelling the lukewarm; some of them said: 'This is a hard saying,' and walked no more with him. His teaching, if we are to trust the gospels, promised to bring us into perfect harmony with God and God's universe, but it never implied that this would save us from fightings without and fears within, until the final harmony had been reached. 'I came not to send peace, but a sword'; 'My peace I give unto you; not as the world giveth, give I unto you'; 'If thine eye offend thee, pluck it out' (Matt. x. 34; John xiv. 27; Mark ix. 47). And this has always been recognized, to do them justice, by the best exponents of that exclusivism which I am asking you, provisionally at least, to cast aside. If traditionalism be, in a sense, our enemy, yet at least it is the first condition of our victory that we should recognize its virtues, and learn from it for ourselves. Here, again, I may appeal to words spoken at Cambridge, in a university sermon which probably impressed some others here present as deeply as it impressed me. The preacher, exhorting us most fervently to follow Christ through the church, not only made no attempt to disguise the difficulties of the

way, but rather dwelt upon them, just as the best monastic
disciplinarians emphasized the hardness of the rule to the
novice, lest he should say afterwards that he had irre-
vocably committed himself to austerities only half-
realized. The preacher concluded: 'It has been said that,
while the highwaymen's cry was *Your money or your life,*
Christ demands *Your money and your life.*'...'The surrender' he added, 'is hard at first; and in some ways it
grows harder from day to day'...; and so on, in few words,
but those so direct and impressive that they were felt to
be a whole sermon in themselves. And this, I think, has
been the way of all men who have moved the world.
Certainly it was Christ's way. The writer of the Epistle to
the Hebrews, again, makes no attempt to minimize the
renunciation for which he pleads, nor artificially to exalt
the convert's gain by disguising the beauty or respectability of the Jewish traditions which the Christian must
forsake. St Francis, like many others in the middle ages,
even deliberately weighted the burden of human renunciation; and he succeeded only in virtue of his own personal
victory over the commonplace; men were converted because they saw him doing the hardest thing in the world as
easily and cheerfully as if it had been the lightest thing in
the world. In so far as he and his followers failed, it was
because they did not cast off all spiritual superfluities as
relentlessly as they cast off the superfluities of earth. Their
attempt literally to imitate Christianity will be depreciated
only by those who have not read sympathetically the early
Franciscan story; but to admit that this imitation was
limited and imperfect is only to confess that the men were
very human after all. Amid all St Francis's anxiety to
share even Christ's bodily sufferings in the most literal
sense, there was one way in which he and his disciples
lacked that full experience of Christ and his little band
which makes the Gospels into such a complete epitome of
human life. Their spiritual renunciation was in no way

commensurate with their material renunciations. When it is urged upon us nowadays, in all friendliness, 'The way of liberty that you claim will be found cold and uncomfortable,' do our advisers bear in mind those words which the Fourth Evangelist puts into Christ's mouth (John xvi. 7)? 'It is expedient for you that I go away: for if I go not away, the Comforter will not come unto you.' Before the crucifixion, no disciple understood the Master's real mission, although it appeared afterwards that he had spoken plainly enough. Seeing so near in the body, he had yet been far from them in spirit:

'Earth, these solid stars, this weight of body and limb,
Are they not sign and symbol of thy division from Him?'

The apostles said to themselves: 'we have God, because the Master is daily here with us; our eyes may see, our hands may handle.' Their later mind, the mind of the Holy Spirit, was rather 'God is tenfold with us now; for all that we truly learned from his Christ is living tenfold still within us, though we no longer can handle him with our hands.' Their second faith was the faith that dieth no more; death had no more dominion over that kingdom of heaven. The Christ of their first and duller hearts, the Christ shrouded in their own imperfect humanity, must needs die, or the Christ as Christ is could never have been revealed. Their comfortable faith, before it could put on incorruption, must needs pass by Christ's way, and cry: *It is finished!!...My God, my God, why hast thou forsaken me?* To hasten that moment, to bring it on wilfully, would be spiritual suicide; but we are not followers of Christ if we shrink from it when it does come, except for that inevitable petition *Father, if thou wilt, let this cup pass away from me!* Why do preachers so seldom emphasize that astounding promise of Jesus when he was rebuking the apostles for their earthly ambitions? (Mark x. 38) 'Ye know not what ye ask: can ye drink of the cup that I drink of? and be

baptized with the baptism that I am baptized with? And
they said unto him: We can. And Jesus said unto them,
Ye shall indeed drink of the cup that I drink of; and with
the baptism that I am baptized withal shall ye be baptized.' Their worldly ambitions were wrong: but in things
purely spiritual no man can be too ambitious. We may
only too truly say 'I dare not,' but Christ himself forbids
us to say 'I cannot.'

In Renan's classical autobiography, amid some flippancy
and some wilful paradox, there is a word which is not
flippantly paradoxical. Writing of his mental struggles,
he says 'Christ seemed to say "leave me, to follow me
truly[62]."'

Certainly, if Socrates and Simmias call upon us as men
to face the austerest truths, it is as Christians that Jesus
bids us face them. Herein is Christianity, not that we
worship a Christ made with our own hands, nor again the
Christ of mere herd-instinct as apart from that higher
society of struggling souls, known only to God, who in all
ages have been the real church—not that we should
worship these, but that we should follow him who died
because he dared to see the truth and to speak the
truth.

St Francis stripped himself of all earthly possessions,
down to the smallest things, in order that nothing might
hinder his course; naked, he would follow the naked Christ.
Most men say, and, I think, truly, that he somewhat over-
did it here. He was greatest where he was most spon-
taneous; the root-idea was splendid, but in its exaggeration
it became forced and mechanical. Reaction came; and too
many friars (as orthodox contemporaries assure us) lived
easier and more idly in the friary than they would have
done in the world. And meanwhile this apostle of renunciation ignored—what it was scarcely possible that any
man should have seen clearly in those days—that we must
cast away not only our financial inheritance but a great deal

of our mental inheritance also, if we are to follow the real Christ. St Francis's rule and testament gave the friar no spiritual freedom commensurate with the liberty secured by his poverty; he was bound to strict conformity with the Roman church. Yet no more was needed than a natural extension of the original principle. One friar of the first generation complained to another that he had been ill-treated; the emperor had banished him for no fault of his own. The other replied: 'Banished!...Who can banish a friar? You built your true home in heaven; who can banish you from that?' The same freedom, and a wider freedom still, comes in all times to those who are conscious of having striven to put away the spiritual weights that do so easily beset us. The Spirit of God, the Holy Spirit, is the unencumbered spirit; in that spirit we are secure against loss, since all abandonment of the perishable must be pure gain; we are strong in that Pauline word 'as having nothing, and yet possessing all things.' Whatsoever we have lost was of the earth, earthy, and we have gained the Lord from heaven[63].

We must take the case only of those who are honestly trying to find God; for I have already hinted that, if we are to emphasize insincerities on both sides, the balance may not be in favour of traditionalism. Here, as in the question of money, we do but defeat our own purpose if we renounce in a mechanical or exaggerated spirit; it is always better to keep, and use wisely, rather than to cast too hastily away. But, with this reservation, it is idle to tell the honest seeker that he will find for all his pains a cold and uncomfortable creed, too meagre to live by. There is plenty in it to live by, if we will only live up to it. The life of a creed is not in its extensiveness but in its intensity. Of all New Testament writers, does not the intensest heat of conviction breathe from St Paul, who had most consciously and deliberately cast away all his spiritual inheritance except that which is common to Judaism and

Christianity? If he had shrunk from going out into the cold, should we ever have known of his very existence? Was it not precisely because the apostle had cut himself away from so much, and at such a cost to the flesh, that he was eternally assured of the truth of all that still remained? Having chosen finally to live by the things which acquiescence could never have counselled, having come to this belief through a catastrophic change, and possessing it thus as bone of his bone and flesh of his flesh, St Paul was inspired to proclaim that most triumphant confession of faith in all world-literature (Rom. viii. 35–9) '*Who shall separate us from the love of Christ? shall tribulation, or distress, or persecution, or famine, or nakedness, or peril, or sword? (as it is written, For thy sake we are killed all the day long; we are accounted as sheep for the slaughter). Nay, in all these things we are more than conquerors through him that loved us. For I am persuaded, that neither death, nor life, nor angels, nor principalities, nor powers, nor things present, nor things to come, nor height, nor depth, nor any other creature, shall be able to separate us from the love of God, which is in Christ Jesus our Lord.*'

# VII

THE fourth objection has still to be met, not simply by pointing out that it is utterly inconsistent with the third, but separately, on its own merits. We are often told that modernism in Christianity is a 'soft option,' 'a line of least resistance,' which men choose as a refuge from the austere gospel of traditionalism. Modernists (to use a word which is at least brief and convenient) are daily accused of cheapening the gospel. Men tell us: 'You will never win the world by lowering the standard of religion; hold up before men's eyes a real sacrifice, and they may come with you, offer them the mockery of a sacrifice, and they will mock at it and you.' The words are very true; but the implication is very false. Nobody ever cheapened the gospel more shamelessly than the traditionalist friar of later generations, of whom both orthodox and unorthodox contemporaries report that he would help you through any sin in the decalogue if you would help him to violate his vow of poverty. On the other hand, no modernist writings I happen to have read would seem to justify even a momentary suspicion that the modernist hopes to get the kingdom of heaven on cheaper terms than other people. I speak again, of course, only of the sincere enquirer; for it must sadly be admitted that insincerity can shroud itself under the cloak of modernism almost as easily as under that of traditionalism. To the sincere modernist all life must be a fight, even an up-hill fight; Christ promises rest to the weary, but at the same time the kingdom of heaven suffereth violence, and the violent take it by force.

After struggling and failing, after struggling and succeeding (to borrow those words of Newman's) each man may at last find his own vision of Christ. It will seldom be St Paul's Damascus-vision; it will come like the dawn, we often scarcely know how, except that a few hours ago it was not, and now it is. And the day, when it comes, may prove dull or rainy, windy or cold; but those who have any faith in Christ at all, and in the Father whom Christ came to reveal, and in the Spirit of Christ as doing far more for us than we can do for ourselves—those men can no more doubt that the answer will come in Christ's own way to the honest seeking soul, than we can doubt of to-morrow's dayspring. He told us to seek, to knock at the closed door. When is the world deaf to the priest with his spiritual message? Is it not when we feel that he himself is not seeking with us? when his teaching is inextricably inter-mingled with things which we fear will not bear the dry light of scientific research; when we are therefore com-pelled to doubt lest even his words of comfort and faith may prove an outworn parrot-song. On the other hand, when are we impressed, in spite of ourselves, by the materialism of scientific extremists? When we note how patiently, how conscientiously they labour in their own field, and how richly in that field they reap the fulfilment of Christ's promise: 'Seek, and ye shall find.'

And to us he says: *Seek ye the kingdom of God....The kingdom of God is ἐντὸς ὑμῶν*—it matters little to the present purpose whether we are to translate that 'within you' or 'among you.' In any case 'closer is it than breathing, and nearer than hands and feet.' The kingdom of God is the state of those men who face honestly their own inward and outward experience, asking themselves at every turn 'what do these things mean to me in the light of the world-long conflict of good and evil?'...'Love ye one another'—'He that loveth his life shall lose it'—'Ye shall find rest unto your souls'—'I am the light of the world'— how far do I find these words borne out or contradicted by all that I have felt and heard and seen, when once I set about to study them, and myself, and my neighbour with the patient sincerity of the scientist at his microscope?

Where the words attract me, is it only because they bring
a flattering feeling of ease? where they repel me, is it
because my severer conscience condemns them, or is it
for the very different reason that they call for an effort to
which I believe myself unequal? The scientist, when he
has strained his eyes to-day into hopeless weariness, knows
very well that the failure was in his own faculties, and
tries again to-morrow until he has convinced himself that
at last he sees up to the limits of human eyesight, or at
least to the limits of his own. How many of us put that
*improbum laborem* into the question 'Art thou he that
should come, or do we look for another?' How many
bring all possible accuracy to the analysis of all the
spiritual elements which lie ἐντὸς ἡμῶν—*within us* or
*among. us*? The real seeker after God's kingdom—the
scientific seeker we may call him—treasures all his higher
impulses; but he faces the lower, and even his actual sins
and follies, just as unflinchingly. He can keep hold, if only
in memory and in desire, upon a youth innocent in so far
as it was ignorant; in later days of conscious conflict, he
can weigh results and analyse their contributory causes;
he utilizes even the waste products of life; struggling and
failing teaches him more, perhaps, than struggling and
success. Is this, then, an easy option, compared with the
life of the man who feels that he has the church as a
mediator and support between him and the unapproach-
able exemplar? None of us will be so unjust as to forget
that, to many of these men whose doctrines we may repudiate, the spiritual struggle of churchmanship is so great,
and the victory in their souls so complete, that we can only
wish we were like them[64]. But we are not pitting individual
against individual; ideal is on its trial against ideal; and
what honest man can venture to say, *a priori*, that we are
lowering the religious ideal by telling the Christian to go
straight to Christ and always to Christ? If you will read
Luther's *Table Talk*, or the autobiography which Michelet

collected out of this and similar personal confessions from
Luther's writings, you will see that his spiritual struggles
were as great as St Augustine's or Newman's; again, nonconformists like Bunyan and Richard Baxter wrestled with
these things as bravely as that university preacher who
warned us that Christ demanded our money *and* our life.

There is, however, something safer than any *a priori*
criterion; we have Christ's own test, the inductive test;
'By their fruits ye shall know them.' The Anglo-catholic
revival began in 1834. For every fifty Anglican priests
who now hold theories on church and ministry and succession closely resembling those of the Roman catholics,
nobody would maintain that England possessed more than
one at that earlier date. Those theories, therefore (quite
apart from their popularity in the middle ages), have had
nearly three generations to manifest their divine nature
in Great Britain, if divine it be. Is anybody sanguine
enough to assert that these three generations have strengthened the church's hold on the nation, or brought better
candidates for holy orders from the universities, or
hastened moral and intellectual progress within the
Anglican church as compared with other churches? The
Archbishops' Report renders it unnecessary to prove in
detail that, if we are to proclaim any change at all, it is a
change for the worse.

But this is a small field, both in space and in time: let us
take the widest possible generalization. For more than
three centuries nearly the whole of Europe has been
divided into catholic and protestant states; what differences can we find here? Such differences are not overwhelming, when we appeal to the cold evidence of statistics.
They point in general to what I have already hinted, that
God meant the search for truth to be hard, so that the best
men are often divided in opinion. We see, as we might
expect, that God is likely to reveal himself more completely
where there is free interchange of thought than when large

Christian bodies are kept 'pure'—i.e. separated from other
Christians by mutually exclusive statements of principle
which may turn out to be neither fundamental nor even
accurate. Purely catholic states do not furnish the best
moral testimonials for catholicism, nor purely protestant
states for protestantism. To begin with statistics of illegitimate births. These are subject in detail, of course, to
all sorts of exceptional considerations before we can weigh
them fairly; yet these exceptions do roughly cancel each
other out if we throw all the details together into the
widest possible field of generalization; and here, on the
whole, the figures show a clear percentage in favour of
protestantism[65]. Secondly, we find the same results with
crime of almost every sort; not only (as is sometimes
asserted) with hot-blooded and passionate crimes. You
may work out these two matters for yourselves in the
official figures printed in *The Statesman's Year-Book*.
Thirdly, though it is not fair to emphasize the enormous
difference in material prosperity between catholic and
protestant states, yet most of us may agree with Dr John-
son that man is seldom more innocently employed than in
making money. But, fourthly, the statistics of education
are, on the whole, just as overwhelmingly in favour of the
protestants. Fifthly, again, anti-clericalism is almost unknown among us in the forms which it assumes in all
Roman catholic countries; French and Italian observers
in Britain are astounded to find many socialists and a host
of freemasons who are Christians. It may safely be asserted that, if the statistics of British illegitimacy or crime
began suddenly to conform, only for a year or two, to the
average statistics of Roman catholic countries, we should
at once appoint a Government commission to discover the
cause and the remedy. If our educational statistics suddenly fell to that level, we might talk of stronger measures
still.

To this we must add the fact that the Roman catholic

church has never repudiated her official theory of persecution. She has never recanted her claim that a baptized
Christian who does not turn to catholicism, after a fair hearing of the Roman case, can escape his liability to the death
penalty only on the plea of invincible ignorance; that is,
not only of present ignorance, but of natural incapacity to
understand these things[66].

On the other hand, early in this war, Anglo-catholics
seized the opportunity of tracing German savagery to
protestantism. But the percentage of Roman catholics
in Germany, and even in Prussia, is almost double that
of the United Kingdom. Moreover, the official British
report has since made it plain that there was nothing to
choose in bestiality between Prussian protestants and
Bavarian catholics, even in the matter of priest-murder
and sacrilege; indeed, I have heard on good authority
that the worst desecrations of churches, in all this war,
were perpetrated by Austrian catholics in Serbia. *The
Church Times* still tries to make capital out of the old
delusion; and whatsoever is written in *The Church Times*
is mechanically repeated from many of our pulpits; but
this war has brought no sound evidence against the general
conclusion that there never has been an age or a place in
which men lived more respectable lives than in modern
protestant Britain or America, and very seldom so respectable.

Let us not unduly emphasize these comparisons; but the
enquiry, in general, is prescribed as clearly by Christ's own
command as by science and common-sense. And, without
giving us cause for pharisaical exultation, the results seem
to leave no room whatever for the notion that 'catholicity'
of doctrine on the subject of church, ministry and succession has contributed more than rival doctrines to the moral
or educational progress of humanity. The non-catholic
course seems not only the harder and more manly way of
life, but the more moral also, so far as we can see our path

clearly through the errors and failures which are only too conspicuous on both sides.

If, then, we can render all these clear reasons for our venture of faith, what shall we say of those who not only refuse to share it, but deny even our right to make it?

If schism there be, are not these the true schismatics[67]? They separate themselves from a vast mass of Christians on grounds which claim to be historical, but which are repudiated by the majority of historians, and are by no means unconditionally approved even by scholars of pronounced catholic sympathies. They refuse all common understanding on a plea which is certainly not approved by *all* Christians *everywhere*, and which (to use the mildest terms) cannot prove itself to have been held *always* by any section whatever of Christ's followers. Their own test of *semper, ubique, ab omnibus* fails them utterly here.


But I have dwelt enough and perhaps more than enough on the several arguments of those who would dissuade us from that venture of faith to which the man in the trenches challenges the churches. Let us pass on to something less negative.

One possible consideration I have already put forward; the modernist is convinced that he is walking, with God's help, in the way of Christ and St Paul and the earliest church. Read the Epistle to the Hebrews; keep in mind the at least conceivable possibility that traditional Christianity, like traditional Judaism, may be weighted down with its past honours and petrified in its age-long respectability; and then you will realize how the modernist feels himself to be not destroying, but unburying and recovering all those things in virtue of which the early Christian was not the man of a great past, but the heir to an infinite future. You will see how there are times when even the most time-honoured doctrines and ceremonies must be spiritualized to preserve them from natural corruption.

The second consideration I would put before you is that, whereas there never was a more democratic religion than real Christianity, much that now shelters itself under that name is repugnant to liberty, equality, and fraternity, in the best sense of those words. This war has been a struggle of democracy against despotism; in spite of much baser alloy, the essential contrast has been clear enough. And, unless despotism can secure a victory, or a drawn battle, in the field, we may safely predict of the ensuing period of reconstruction that it will bring immense democratic progress. It can scarcely seem rash to conclude that either the church will be greatly democratized, or democracy will repudiate the church[68]. We look forward, then, to growing democracy in religion. We are content in church as in state to accept the risks of democracy, if only we can secure its redeeming virtues. To the comforts of benevolent despotism—comforts which are very real for many others besides the most privileged classes—we must say good-bye, and put out upon a greater sea of spiritual adventure. Without blaming those who held back in the past, we shall feel convinced that all further hesitations, at this moment, would be prompted not by faith but by unfaith. We have now the experience of many generations behind us; this is no leap in the dark, but a steady and measured torch-light progress which will scatter the shadows before our advance. The man from the trenches, with whom we hope to cooperate, represents the people in its most real form.

The strength of the Franciscan movement was its direct appeal to the multitude. Ozanam, writing of St Francis's poetry, says very truly 'he sought poetry where it was to be found, among the people.' There also religion is to be found; potentialities of religion, if only we could awaken them, infinitely beyond the religious actualities of the official church. Even the most careless men know in their hearts, that certain things are to be apprehended by faith alone; and they are willing to strive after such faith— languidly enough, perhaps at ordinary times, but often unexpectedly and passionately anxious to apprehend it at moments of stress like these[69]. We hope to raise the educational standard by enlisting the wider forces of democracy; and on that road lies our religious salvation also. A double movement is needed here; of creation and of communication. The specialist s studies become more and more complicated, and therefore more and more specialized, as civilization advances; but, necessary as this specialization is, it is just as important that the growing heritage of specialist thought should be formulated in simple terms to the multitude; and it needs as rare a genius for one task as for the other. Christianity was once the. simplest, even while it was the most comprehensive of religious ideas. How much of that essential simplicity has it retained? The early Christian's heart overflowed; 'Woe is me, if I preach not the gospel.' In our own day, on the contrary, the greatest theologians are often the most reticent. Lord Acton was a great theologian as well as a great historian; to how many people on this earth would he have said frankly what he thought of Loisy? In Loisy himself, the reticence is almost as marked as the outspoken boldness. We must strive for the people's sake to simplify our formulas of Christian belief. If that which the churches hold for the essence of Christianity be indeed incapable of simple and convincing formulation, then we are still living in an age like that of Wyclif, when the average thinking man's religion was so graphically portrayed by the author of *Piers Plowman*. The sincere soul in that poem, after clinging as long as possible to the traditional fold, finds himself compelled at last to shake the dust of it from his feet, and to go forth into the wilderness in search of the Christ that is to be. Five generations after this poem, came the most violent religious revolution that has ever convulsed Christendom. If we shrink from reasonable democratic reform in Christianity, we shall finally get the unreasoning religious Bolshevik; and, worst of all, we shall have thoroughly deserved him. Exclusivism has the strength and the weakness of Imperial Germany; its powers of resistance up to a certain point are marvellous; but a serious failure brings utter and irremediable ruin.

This seems the moment to return to a point which I have tried to keep before you all along, but which must be put beyond all risk of ambiguity, even at the expense of wearisome reiteration. It might have seemed, at first sight, as if this plea of ours for a fresh start on common Christian ground·were really a quiet begging of the whole question. Traditionalists will say (as they said in that unhappy controversy about religious teaching in schools) "The Christianity for which you plead is no Christianity at all: you are asking us to give up our faith for the sake of fraternizing with you.'

But I hope you will already have realized that we ask no such thing. We ask something very different, that they should no longer claim historical certainty for mere pious opinions; that they should bring themselves to a frame of mind which recognizes the unwisdom, and even the iniquity of dogmatizing about matters which our Lord seems to have left open; and finally, that they should show faith in their own professed creed[70].

If I have spoken throughout as one personally convinced of the emptiness of many current theories about church and ministry and succession—if I have urged against those theories arguments which to myself seem conclusive—this is only my right and my bounden duty; I plead here for thousands of educated people whom dogmatism no longer satisfies, and who can be converted only by reason on the ground common to most reasonable men. But such common ground can be found only where both sides have consented, hypothetically and *ad interim*, to sink their

preconceived differences. This is what most of us have
been doing to win the war. The radical does not ask the tory
to give up his tory convictions, but to work with him on
common ground; and *vice versa*. The pacifist, who is convinced that the whole thing is a ghastly blunder and crime,
and whose doctrines, if true, would forbid him in conscience
to cooperate at all in the struggle against Germany—the
pacifist, I say, whose convictions tempt him here to a
dogmatism equal to that of the extreme militarist in
politics, or the extreme catholic in religion, does nevertheless do his best to argue the question on common ground.
The early Christians were expressly bidden to have reasons
for the faith that was in them; a party that refuses to
reason is a dead or dying party. But no appeal to reason
is possible unless traditionalist, as well as modernist, will
admit the theoretical possibility that he is, after all, in the
wrong, and that the search for truth might, after all, bring
him over to the other side. Therefore, I am only pleading
that, for truth's sake (or, in other words, for Christ's sake),
we should all start from no preconceived assumption that
the congregationalist theory of church organization and
authority must necessarily be totally wrong, or that the
unitarian must be totally wrong in his conception of
physical miracles. We must all admit the possibility, at
least, that the final truth may prove to be more on the
other side than we at present think. This is not only the
one conceivable way to unity—as the evidence from the
trenches shows—but it is the only morally justifiable
attitude. The man who calls upon others to follow his
lead unquestioningly in the highest matters that humanity
can deal with, is in effect claiming infallibility. He does
not mend matters by saying it is the church which is infallible, so long as he persists in defining the church
as the body of those who think with himself; and this,
in the last analysis, is what the strict catholic theory
comes to. There is little difference between the theory

of individual infallibility and that of infallibility in
partnership.

I am asking no man therefore, to give up any idea except
this, which would seem absurd on the very face of it.
There is no real sacrifice of conviction in a provisional
*ad interim* admission that the congregationalist or unitarian may possibly be partly right; it is only a frank
admission of what everybody takes for granted in every
department of human thought except theology. Every
man, at the bottom of his heart, believes in the possibility
of serious error, though it is fairly easy to work oneself
into a state of mind in which we think we believe otherwise. When once it is admitted that the real truth may
lie somewhere between two parties, however much nearer
to our side than the other, then it would seem to follow as
a moral duty that no claim of individual or corporate
infallibility should be allowed to veto that interchange of
thoughts which common sense seems to demand of both
parties. And, if others are willing to worship reverently
with us, or if circumstances render it natural for us to
kneel reverently with them, let us look upon this as a gift
of God, not as a snare of the devil. The idea that, by thus
fraternizing, we shall lose more than we gain, seems a
subtle but fatal form of infidelity. If truth be truth, what
better opportunity can it have than to be confronted with
error under the conditions which do most to disarm error?
When a trinitarian finds himself kneeling with a unitarian
to say the Lord's prayer; when both repeat together, with
only the ordinary and average sincerity of liturgical
routine, *thy kingdom come, thy will be done,* who can
reasonably doubt that each is thereby attuned to a better
comprehension of such truth as the other may have
realized? Infinitely stronger is the case where the presbyterian begs permission to commemorate the last supper
with us. If all truth be indeed on our side, can there be
any more providential opportunity than this for bringing

him to all truth? Is not the Holy Spirit supreme here? and
is it not flat sin against the Holy Ghost to see evil even in
good, when it happens to be our adversary's good? Those
who keep their fellow-Christians at arm's length in the
conviction that such common worship would more en-
danger their own faith than it would raise the (*ex hypothesi*) lower faith of the nonconformist, should recite
weekly or daily in their creed 'I disbelieve in the Holy
Ghost.' So long as they persistently avoid common
Christian ground, and, by their own confession, are afraid
of it, they will necessarily petrify more and more in that
sectarian spirit which they so deliberately cherish as a
virtue.

Catholics of all schools need to remember that sentence
which their medieval forefathers were wont to quote so
liberally, yet with so much less immediate appositeness,
against the heretic: 'qui ignorat, ignorabitur' (1 Cor. xiv.
38 *Vulg.*). A sect, or, perhaps, only the minority of a sect,
stiffening more and more into the impossibility of interchange with other Christians, must some day stand in
confessed isolation, and therefore (according to the majoritarian theory) of heresy; given this impossible policy, the
result is only a question of time. But I say advisedly, *only
the minority of a sect*, since this spirit of extreme isolation
began to show signs of breaking down even before the war.
For some time, at any rate, the most learned catholics
have often shown themselves least afraid of taking the
protestant on his own ground; and a representative French
protestant like the late Gabriel Monod confessed frankly
that Loisy's apologia for catholicism was far more difficult
to meet than those of the old school, which in these days
provoke only a smile.

Let us see, then, what this *ad interim* concordat would
mean. For church, ministry, and succession it would mean
the admission to full church worship of everyone who shows
a sincere wish to join reverently in such ceremonies. It

would mean that priest and congregation would have far
greater liturgical latitude—a latitude rendering it possible
for both modernist and extreme Anglo-catholic to go as
far, each in his own direction, as they could carry their
congregations with them. For the so-called Apostles'
Creed, the Nicene Creed and the so-called Creed of St
Athanasius we should be free to substitute what the
Churchmen's Union has suggested as St John's Creed:

'We believe that God is Spirit, and they that worship
him must worship him in spirit and in truth.

'We believe that God is Light, and that if we walk in the
light as he is in the light, we have fellowship one with
another.

'We believe that God is Love, and that everyone that
loveth is born of God and knoweth God.

'We believe that Jesus is the Son of God, and that God
has given to us eternal life, and this life is in his son.

'We believe that we are children of God, and that he hath
given us of his spirit.

'We believe that if we confess our sins, he is faithful and
just to forgive us our sins.

'We believe that the world passeth away, and the lust
thereof, but he that doeth the will of God abideth for ever.'

This, of course, would involve similar alternatives elsewhere in the services. Such changes can seem revolutionary
only to those who do not take account of what is actually
going on at the present moment. The Anglo-catholic
priest, in perhaps the majority of cases, keeps the congregation waiting while he recites *sotto voce* some pre-
reformation mass-prayer which the reforming compilers
deliberately omitted from the service of the church of
England. In some cases, it is notorious that the priest
thus repeats the whole canon of the Roman mass while his
Anglican congregation wait on their knees. The modernist
priest, and many people in every congregation, recite the
traditional creeds with mental reservations which are even

more alien to the spirit of the prayer-book compilers. We are only asking, therefore, that the church should boldly face the facts, and recognize the superior morality of doing openly what is now done more or less furtively on almost every side. If, under such freedom, priests and people could not manage to agree in Christ, then we should doubtless have disestablishment. But, surely, the present state of things points also to disestablishment, under conditions far less honourable to the church. The public will not always continue to tolerate a religious body in which things are frequently and notoriously done secretly which it would seem revolutionary to do openly before the face of God and man. The longer this underground ferment continues, the worse must be the explosion.

But this is only anticipating the worst, if it must come to the worst. Meanwhile any sincere concordat would involve occasional interchange of pulpits, and far more frequent meetings of churchmen and nonconformists on common ground. Far higher work, it may confidently be predicted, would be found for women, and we should no longer have the scandal that, if a woman wishes to speak on religious subjects, and large numbers of people want to hear her, they must needs find some unconsecrated building, and squeeze into the village schoolroom while the great church stands empty. But all these changes would only supplement existing arrangements. Those who disdain to hear a woman in church or who look upon the Pauline sentence as conclusive, would continue then, as now, to find their full spiritual food in the ordinary services. Any one who could get his people to assent to it would still be free to recite, in the words falsely attributed to St Athanasius, that all who disagree with them as to certain very abstract doctrines 'will without doubt perish everlastingly.' The episcopalian would still be free to believe in his heart that episcopacy is not only the best church system yet evolved, but the only divinely-appointed

system. He would be free to avoid nonconformist places
of worship as much as he chose.  Moreover, those to whom
the presence of a presbyterian at holy communion seemed
an intolerable defilement, might be left perfectly free to
form within the Anglican church a community of their
own, hedged round by the strictest exclusivism. Here, as
elsewhere, the conscientious objector should be left as
much as possible to his own peculiar objections.

For the rest, none of the new would supersede the old
unless and as far as circumstances evidently called for the
change. Country clergy constantly complain that it is
difficult to compose some 120 sermons a year, and to go on
saying fresh things to their people. The congregations
often agree with them; and, if it becomes obvious to both
sides that the sermons become more living under a wider
system of pulpit-interchange than under the strict conception of apostolical succession, then we shall get the
best unity of all, that of common consent on the basis of
common sense. The lay preacher and the nonconformist
colleague, under such circumstances as these, will en-
croach upon the old routine just so far as they have
justified this encroachment in practice.

The plea that we should all be prepared to treat physical
miracles as strictly secondary to the moral miracle of
Christianity may naturally arouse more serious misgiving.
It would not only mean that, at the Eucharist, we should
have men who accept the real presence in a sense scarcely
distinguishable from transubstantiation, kneeling side by
side with others to whom *Body* and *Blood* are only meta-
phors expressive of that intimate spiritual union with
Christ which is created by the solemn and periodical commemoration of his death for us. It is not only that we
should have a good many in every church who refuse to
repeat the so-called Apostles' creed, because they frankly
refuse to accept it in the sense in which it was first drawn
up, long after apostolic times. These things we have

c.                                                        9

already; it is a phenomenon long familiar to clergy and to
laity, and no measures could prohibit it but such as would
intensify the already lamentable depletion of our churches.
More than this, however, would happen under the wider
Christian life for which I am pleading. Theological tests
would be relaxed; there would be no more solemn professions of agreement with those Thirty-nine Articles of
which some, at least, are incredible in their ordinary sense
to the high churchman, others to the low, and others to the
broad, so that there is scarcely a priest who accepts them
all with heartfelt sincerity [71]. There would be far greater
diversity of doctrine in sermons. There would probably be
considerable friction at first; perhaps even as much friction
as in that lamentable quarrel between church and nonconformity about religious teaching which ended logically
in the banishment of the Bible from our schools. It would
unquestionably be a venture of faith. There would be as
much difference of opinion, even between preacher and
preacher, as there was between the Peter who rebuked
Christ for speaking of his coming death and the Peter of
after Pentecost; or as there was between those first three
centuries in which the trinitarian question was still open,
and the centuries after Nicea, when it had been officially
closed. We might even have one archbishop withstanding
another to his face, as St Paul withstood St Peter on the
still greater exclusion question of Jew or Gentile. Yet,
even as a purely political problem, this might not prove
altogether insoluble. Why then, should it seem hopeless
as a gospel effort [72]? Even politically, the way has been
prepared for it by the trend of modern thought, especially
since 1914. All men who believe not only in Christ but also
in a possible league of nations, however tentative, ought
to find no difficulty here. True church feeling would be no
more extinguished by our realizing its ideal in a church of
churches, than democratic feeling would suffer from a
federation of existing democracies. Yet that political

federation is already a fact; and we now see no reason why the French republic, one and indivisible, should not work harmoniously both with the federal republics of America and Switzerland, and with the monarchical republic of Great Britain. These political bodies work together, because they emphasize their agreement on democratic principle, and can afford to ignore differences of detail. The general tendency of modern times to solve acute political differences by federative rather than imperialistic methods has already prepared most minds for the possibility that the seamless robe of Christ may be also a coat of many colours, and that the real road to unity may lie in a union less of bodies than of hearts. We must not neglect the former; on the contrary, let us have as much of it as possible. Mr H. G. Wells, in his *God the Invisible King*, freely admits that all men ought to pray, and that most people are stronger for praying sometimes in unison; in other words, that a visible church must always be our aim. The general irritation against modern exclusivism, as a hobby which is so often ridden·hardest by the most insignificant churchmen, has tended to unjust forgetfulness of all that the pre-reformation church and the post-reformation churches have done for Europe in the past. For centuries, the cleric was the main civilizing influence; at the worst of times, average clerical morality was at least some degrees superior to that of the average layman, and few fair-minded men who know both parties intimately will be inclined to deny that it is so still. It was a convinced agnostic, Mr Havelock Ellis, whose scientific statistical studies in *The Dictionary of National Biography* brought out the fact that the sons of the clergy have come to the fore in the proportion of nearly three to one, as compared even with other learned professions such as the law and medicine[73]. Personally, after long and sceptical observation in several European countries and among very different social classes, I am equally convinced that the conduct of the average professing Christian is sensibly higher than that of the average civilized non-Christian. The idea of a necessary church, and the reverence for that church, could scarcely fail to increase under any system which would give free play to both the individualism and the collectivism which are natural to man. But the deepest reverence of all will always be felt for that church upon which St Augustine fell back whenever his narrower definitions were too obviously unsatisfactory—the society of the elect—of those who are certainly known to God alone, but to some extent recognizable among their fellow-men by their personal obedience to Christ's commands and their insistence upon those essentials which alone can secure spiritual unity amid the infinite multitude and diversity of human minds. If the spirit of Christ is alive among modern Christians—if, among our twenty millions of adult British population, there are just twenty thousand ready to shape the whole course of their lives on the public profession and inward guidance of Christ above all—then, even though the new reformation were as devoid of political organization as the Society of Friends always has been, it would at least rival the civilizing influence of that society, which has modified modern thought to an extent quite disproportionate to its numerical membership. But, as we are calling upon the traditionalist for a sacrifice towards this end, still more are we ourselves bound to meet him half way. The ministers of the new reformation cannot, with any enduring success, store the new wine in old bottles; the average layman rightly demands that there should be no doubt as to the sense in which a clergyman uses English words, so far as the abstract difficulty of the subject permits the formulation of clear thoughts in clear language[74]. And the laity themselves must strive not to be outdone by the clergy in all sober imitation of Christ. Congregations which pay their parson to do the praying and preaching and good living for them will get the parsons they deserve. It was not only to the clergy that the apostle said: 'Ye are bought with a price.' Traditionalist and modernist are here in agreement, that the earliest days of missionary fervour in the church were days of slender distinction in zeal between clergy and laity. And have not nearly all the greatest reforming movements in Christianity rested upon a very strong lay element?

Again, whatever may have been the source of the authority which some certainly exercised over others in very early days, it is certain that this authority was commended by the personal worth of those who wielded it. The earliest hierarchical ideal was still Christ's ideal, that higher rank should be chiefly marked by more self-denying service. There is a story told of St Thomas Aquinas which may be only *ben trovato*, but which certainly expresses what men were saying already six centuries ago. He went to see the pope on business, and found him counting out his money. The pope shuffled the coin away with a jest: 'You see, St Peter can no longer say: *silver and gold have I none*.' 'No,' replied St Thomas; 'nor can he now add: *such as I have I give thee; in the name of Jesus Christ of Nazareth rise up and walk*.' There are only two possible lines of proof for the catholic doctrine of apostolical succession; the historical and the moral. Students are perfectly willing to admit the theory if it can be proved by the first of these, i.e. from actual records. On the other hand, the world in general will accept any theory of apostolic legitimacy which is accompanied by a visible manifestation of apostolic power. When that power begins visibly to fail, then it is impossible to stifle doubts as to its historic legitimacy.

# VIII

A$^T$ the end of my last lecture, I reminded you of the Pauline plea, 'ye are bought with a price.' Dr Rashdall has shown us the strange vicissitudes of this Christian doctrine of redemption, which to St Paul is a matter not of argument but of feeling. Origen, and other early fathers, expound the term with crude legal materialism: Adam's sin gave the human race to the devil, and God must be just even to the devil: therefore our souls cannot be bought back except by paying to the devil something more precious than they—Christ's blood[75]. St Anselm, eight hundred years ago, took one decisive step away from this unspiritual conception. Without shaking himself altogether free from the legal theory, he did much to spiritualize it; the dispute, according to him, is not between God and the devil, but between God's justice and God's mercy; and it is Christ's sacrifice which turns the scale. It was Abelard, Anselm's younger contemporary, who finally got rid of the legal conception altogether, and explained redemption as the modernist would explain it to-day. The perfect love shown in that sacrifice, he argues, commands our love in return; Christ's is the supreme example of what Dante afterwards called 'inexorable love'—*amor, che a nullo amato amar perdona*—and the soul that truly loves is a soul redeemed from sin.

This is a conception for which the modern Christian world is ripe. It is not usual to talk much about these things; and certainly a convention of silence is many degrees better than conventional loquacity. Present-day reticence is probably due in part also to that artificial division between clergy and laity which often casts an atmosphere of unreality about religious talk. But all chaplains from the front have borne witness to the wide prevalence, under the surface, of rudimentary and potential Christian ideas; and one of these observers, at least, has been much interested to discover what is at the bottom of many educated men's minds. His testimony amounts to this, that a large proportion of officers think the clergy right enough in the main, yet believe themselves to hold a higher, though vaguer and less articulate faith. You will probably recognize this description as very true; and you will perhaps be rather inclined to wonder why it should have needed a journey to the front to discover what the clergy might have learned any time these thirty years, if only there had been a franker and more sympathetic interchange of thought between them and the more educated portion of their flocks. Those whose work has brought them into close contact with men of many professions will probably recognize the following case as fairly typical. I once knew a business man of very scanty leisure, brother to a well-known university professor now dead. My acquaintance had been brought up in unquestioning belief. In early manhood, he gradually recognized the falsity of certain antiquated religious conceptions which even enlightened Anglo-catholics like the bishop of Oxford have abandoned in our day. But fifty years ago, when this young man cast them off, the so-called teaching church was daily dinning into the ears of the faithful that they must believe these things or nothing; and in those days the reigning bishop of Oxford would have said concerning the present bishop of Oxford's views what *Viator* of *The Church Times* says now concerning the modernist clergy: 'I wish —— and —— would frankly confess that their religion is not that of the Christian church[76].' Those were the days when Liddon wrote his Bampton lectures—perhaps the bulkiest and the most famous of all the long line of Bampton lectures—to prove conclusively that if Christ was not God Almighty he could not even have been a good man. The young man, therefore, having lost his religion, gave up what time he could spare to work among the poor. There he came to the gradual certainty that religion, in one shape or another, is one of the main distinctions between man and beast; and thus, by insensible stages, he arrived again at a creed which, to him, retained all the essentials of that which he had abandoned. In 'his years of unsettlement, his daily doubts about the element of physical miracle in the gospels had kept him in a state of perpetual mental irritation. Even when he had got over the original fear that it was sinful merely to enquire, the constant effort of enquiry was always re-opening his wounds. It was only after he had contemptuously cast aside the miraculous, that his honest desire for truth made him ask seriously whether this was not inverted dogmatism; whether Socrates would not have kept an open mind; and finally, whether the whole mental conflict was not God's way of showing that even the fog of mistaken miracles, if mistaken miracles there be, cannot conceal the saving truth that we are heirs of God, and joint-heirs with Christ, if so be that we suffer with him. The least religious moments of this man's whole life had been the last few months of his earlier conformity to church religion. He had then ceased to pray even when he knelt in public: prayer came back to him many years later, when at last he could feel sure that it was a cry of his own heart and not a mere parrot-lesson. But to such prayer, and to a very real faith, he clung with silent devotion. I have heard him say: 'Nobody can read the 14th and 15th chapters of St John's gospel beside a deathbed, and not feel that those are God's words.' In later life, he came regularly again to church, and few of those who knew him doubted that the church was the better for his presence.

This, then, was one of the best of a large class who are typified on the most intellectual side by Matthew Arnold. In some, these ideas formulate themselves in a more or less definite rival religion, such as Theosophy or Christian

Science. But in most cases, perhaps, the man is willing
to follow traditional forms, so long as he follows any form
at all. Only he goes on with a quiet conviction that he has
got for himself, straight from God, something inherently
better than what he would call a priest-made religion. As
the chaplain complained from whom I have already quoted,
he quietly patronizes the priest in his own mind. For in
fact, little as this faith may be in quantity, in quality it
has the spontaneity of that which we have discovered for
ourselves [77]. Such a man has asked, after his own fashion,
John Baptist's question; Christ has given him the same
answer; and, after weighing the world and his own soul in
obedience to that answer, he has finally decided: *Thou art
he that should come; I look for no other.* All this, perhaps, in
a mere average sort of way, with none of those high professions which the official church so rightly makes in word
and often neglects so culpably in deed; yet let us remember
that God loves the average man; not his low average, but
the man. Organized religion has many virtues; but it is
tempted too often to ignore that 'the kingdom of heaven
is like unto leaven which a woman took and hid in three
measures of meal, till the whole was leavened' (Matt. xiii.
33). We boast very truly that the church has shown her
strength and vitality by the quiet persistence with which,
during these nineteen centuries, she has absorbed fresh
spiritual and intellectual nourishment from the most varied
sources; but we are apt to forget how imperceptible this
process often is at any given moment, and how obscure
also are the springs from which religion is thus fed. Yet is
not the hidden human mind one of the richest of these
sources, if not the richest of all? Has not the church
sucked most of her strength, and her kindliest and whole-
somest nourishment, from those inarticulate millions who
do not talk about religion, but feel it? Officialism is
tempted to ignore this truth, though the really great souls
of the official church have often recognized it, implicitly at

least. In Bossuet, for instance, if we turn away from his formal panegyrics to his more familiar sermons, we find full acknowledgment of the vast though imponderable spiritual forces latent in common humanity. To millions of people who do not talk about it, religion has gradually become a quiet reality. Francis Thompson's *Hound of Heaven* gives too dramatic a description of the way in which God finds very many men; in the vast majority of cases, is it not something more intimate than this? Is it not less a force or a spirit from without than a part of the man's self—a second self, like the second lobe of the brain —which has seen the vision once, and will never now forget?...A mere child of the imagination, someone may suggest....No; it is a child indeed, but not of imagination; a real child of the man's own self, with real and insistent claims upon its progenitor. The child after the flesh transforms the whole lives of its parents; silently and imperceptibly this little thing, scarcely conscious and almost invertebrate in its beginnings, forces the mature organisms around it into a different way of life. At every step it brings in fresh responsibilities, fresh claims, fresh compromises between the independent and the dependent life. By no honest means can it ever thenceforth be got rid of; cast off, it is still there, if only to its deserter's shame. In the vast majority of cases, if we go beyond Christ's parable at all, and conceive of the average man's religion as anything more definite than the secret ferment of the leaven, it is certainly no more definite than that force of parentage which hourly compels the human mind to pass beyond itself to a recognition of the not-self. But what a change even that implies! and what must be the cumulative action of millions of such lives, age after age, upon the growth of the church!

Let us recognize freely, therefore, the sacredness of the average man, as part of the hidden sanctity of the church. Christ has called such an one from his nets or from the

receipt of custom: the man has heard the call, if ever so
dimly, and is following, at however great a distance; he
will never again be quite the same as he was before he
thought seriously of the sacrificed Jesus. He is swept
along, with millions of his fellows, in Christ's great world-
procession; and if others, from their superior standpoint,
would repudiate him altogether because he followeth not
with us, yet Christ all the while takes him to himself: 'he
that is not against us, is for us.' His very imperfections
are partly the reflection of the church's own; the average
man will always follow at a certain distance behind the
elect; nor will it mend matters much if the elect try
periodically to hustle him onwards after the *How now, ye
rebels* fashion. Moreover, if this faith of his seems vague,
we are bound to remember that, other things being equal,
the simplest faith is the strongest. The Jew rose high
above those others who worshipped God in his stars; and
yet, of all idolatries, that would seem the most respectable;
to worship God in the stars of heaven is surely far nobler
than to worship him in a graven image. But the Jew could
worship him apart even from the stars; and, when Judaism
itself became entangled in elaborate ceremonial, the Christian could go beyond this, and worship a spiritual being
whom it seemed sacrilegious to represent visibly; Origen,
speaking for his fellow-Christians, has only contempt for
those men who vainly think that they can raise their
thoughts to God through the image of any visible thing[78].
It is idle to reproach a creed with vagueness, so long as its
votaries fulfil Christ's test: 'by their fruits ye shall know
them.' So far as they grasp firmly principles and motives
which are intangible to us, so far they are better men
than we.

Chaplains, then, are quite correct in their diagnosis; the
officer-class, both in the trenches and in civil life, contains
a large proportion of men who are well-disposed towards
official Christianity, but not at all impressed by the claims

of the church to supreme authority over the individual conscience. For at least a whole generation, this has been growing more evident to all who cared to see it; and the fact itself is of the greatest possible significance. Whithersoever we turn, we find around us souls who seem indifferent only because they are trying to find a better creed than those cut-and-dried medievalisms with which they are being spoon-fed week by week. A large proportion of these men would be willing to assume every responsibility for their own faith if it came to the pinch—and, the sorer the pinch, the more steadfast would they be found. If once the removal of artificial barriers made it possible, if the visible church could be seen staking her future upon the charity that believeth all things and hopeth all things, these men would do very open and very practical homage 'unto him that loved us, and washed us from our sins in his own blood, and hath made us kings and priests unto God and his Father' (Rev. i. 5); for they know already in their hearts that they are bought with a price. We should then regain that living conception of every Christian as a potential priest which breathes so strongly from the New Testament. Church conformity would imply no mere passive acquiescence, but a consciously dedicated life— consciously dedicated in the man's own mind, if not separated by formal outward signs—bearing fruit some an hundredfold, some sixtyfold, some thirtyfold, some perhaps far less, yet ever bearing some real fruit, ever working in silence among that invisible leaven of Christianity which is gradually leavening the world. Every Christian, let us repeat it, would claim that potential priesthood of apostolic times, and all would take to themselves those ordination lines of Keble's, splendid in their quiet sincerity:

'Think not of rest; though dreams be sweet,
Start up, and ply your heavenward feet.
Is not God's oath upon your head,
Ne'er to sink back on slothful bed.

Never again your loins untie,
Nor let your torches waste and die,
Till, when the shadows thickest fall,
Ye hear your Master's midnight call?'

Can we hope to find any more providential moment for seizing again upon this central idea of redemption through Christ's blood, under that most spiritual form wherein time cannot touch it? Most men now confess freely though sadly—a few more confess it reluctantly,'with horror and loathing, hating the truth and yet unable, as honest men, to resist it—but almost every man now confesses, in his own mind, that this war has opened our eyes to many things which, in peace-time, were only too easily ignored. What is more, we know that some of these ignored truths, if they had been boldly faced, might have made this war impossible. If the militarist had trusted God, and the pacifist had kept his powder dry, the Central Powers would never have been tempted into this disastrous adventure Therefore, in the most literal sense, these hundreds of thousands have died as a ransom for sin; since wilful or even careless ignorance are among the most fatal of sins. They have died in order to teach us things which conservatism and self-satisfaction hid from us in the past. We see now that the writing was always on the wall, but we ate and drank and gave in marriage without raising our eyes to it. The soldiers die to redeem that past blindness of society in general, and other still blinder follies of the present; for the two extremes of Pan-Germanism and Bolshevism are only typical of the disastrous, though less glaring extremes of unregenerate self-will in every country; and these unreasonable extremists, even when they do not work formally together as in Russia, are in practice allied everywhere by their joint campaign against patient common sense. Thousands have died for Lenin's and Trotzky's unbalanced minds; thousands more for the skulking profiteer; thousands, again, because even now men will not face the truth which was so frankly stated by the great quaker banker and historian Thomas Hodgkin, that if Christ absolutely forbade war, then he forbade banking also, since all who amass property (whether they confess it to themselves or not) are dependent upon other men's physical force to protect it[79]. Truths like this, in every department of life, have long been plain to a minority, but it has needed a ghastly war to make the majority realize them. Nothing but blood could compel the heedless to say at last: 'These things are so patently false, and in some cases so loathsomely false, that we can no longer live with them.'

But this, we may hope, is only the beginning. The stubble and the straw are burnt away, but the rents still remain to be walled up, and the new Jerusalem remains still to be built with a sense of general proportion which has been sadly lacking in recent years. If any man can bring to this task a better spirit than the spirit of Christ, then Christ's own spirit would impel us to welcome that man's cooperation. But, meanwhile, all reports from the trenches seem to agree in this—not only the chaplains but all other thoughtful observers seem to agree—that most men recognize the spirit of Christ as sufficient to redeem the present world, just as it redeemed the world of the barbarian invasions, if only Christian professors will say in word and deed, like Julius Caesar, not 'Go on!' but 'Come on!' William Blake's words, here again, seem as true now as a century ago: 'Man must and will have some religion; if he has not the religion of Jesus he will have the religion of Satan, and will erect the synagogue of Satan, calling the prince of this world "God."' And recent events have made it easier for us to understand the sacrifice of Jesus than any other experience, in this country at least, since the middle ages. Everybody now has grasped, if only in its most rudimentary form, the eternal truth of redemption through unmerited suffering.

It is not right that we should let our minds dwell in
sickly impotence upon the horrors of this war. All those
to whom sex or age or circumstance have forbidden active
participation, have been well advised to work unremit-
tingly at anything else that comes to their hand, if only to
keep their minds in health. Mere ascetic contemplation of
the battlefield, mourning for mourning's sake, is not in the
spirit of modern civilization or of original Christianity.
But there are times when we must hark back in imagination to the worst, to the very worst, in order dimly to
realize what St Paul meant with his 'God forbid! we that
are dead to sin, how shall we live any longer therein?' and
William Blake again, with his apostrophe to evil

> 'The Death of Jesus set me free,
> Then what have I to do with thee?'

and Bossuet's words: 'All redeemed souls are of the same
price in Jesus Christ; and the measure of their value is the
common ransom of his blood[80].' We must think for a
moment of those whom we have personally known, the
best of them, who lie out there. We must remember what
they were enjoying and giving out, and what promise there
was in their future: and how, when each of us has reckoned
up his own personal sum of loss, all this is but a drop in the
ocean of slaughter. And we must go further down than
this. Those who occur to our minds are mostly the officers:
there is a brilliance about their story which partly redeems
the tragedy; some have left us actual writings which will
be read as long as the language endures; even among the
rest we see poetry, though a very bitter poetry, in their
early fate. Look down now to the roots of all this; consider the average man in the trenches, and the unredeemed
drab prose of his sacrifice. Christ was a village carpenter;
think of a common village carpenter among those thousands who went first of all, because we from our platforms
exhorted them by going first to shame the rest; or again,

take one among those other tens of thousands whom we
contemptuously lumped together as 'the rest'; but who
were often so deeply pledged to wife and children and work
that their going meant the loss of everything except
honour. Take these men, whose separate acts of devotion
are buried under their very numbers, and whose sacrifice
was all the more godlike because it was not reflective, not
consciously fortified by the thousand examples that a
leisured man may glean from history, but merely dumb
and instinctive. Literally instinctive: for, if instinct be
the inherited experience of a million generations, then
these martyrs had in them the inherited experience of all
civilization, concordant with Christ's teaching, that by such
self-abandonment the world is gradually redeemed, and he
that loseth his life shall gain it. It is the holocaust of
these common men that we must think of; their pain and
struggles and unrecorded extinction, and Abraham Lin-
coln's immortal saying 'Friend, the Lord prefers common-
looking people, and that is why he made so many of them.'
To the man who has habitually referred everything to the
Christian standard, it is inevitable to reflect that Christ
has been crucified afresh on these battlefields. But again,
to those who have not so thought of Christ hitherto, the
same truth is becoming visible from the other end; they
can now conceive how the single death of Christ summed
up in itself the whole lesson that the million deaths of these
four years have to teach us. And I must here ask you to go
one step further again. We attempt to realize Christ's
death by constant commemoration of the event itself and
all that it means to us. There can be no irreverence in the
attempt to realize it now through the dead or dying soldier
of to-day. I dare even ask you to try to get hold of that
little book of verse in which a French soldier has described,
with a reverent pathos which nobody can fail to recognize
under the comedian's mask that he puts on, the Sufferings
of Brother Tommy the Martyr—*La Passion de Notre Frère*

*Poilu.* If, at the present moment, we were considering this subject not at our ease after an English afternoon tea, but in the shambles of No Man's Land, or in one of the most ghastly wards of a military hospital, with the naked truth besieging our eyes and our ears—and if we chanced to find there some deafened and blinded soldier who had gone into battle with all the carelessness of yesterday, and who had come out of it, as a few do, not sobered but rather more reckless of himself and of others—how utterly, in spite of our compassion for the man himself, should we be revolted by such talk and behaviour amid such surroundings! Yet his talk would be very much the ordinary pre-war talk of every day; and the surroundings, though we can realize this only by a strong effort of imagination, are in effect our surroundings at this moment. To better eyes and ears than ours, the thing is not distant imagination but present fact; we sit among those ghastly realities not within a radius of ten feet, it is true, but within two or three hundred miles, and what is that difference of distance in face of the infinite? In every ward of those hospitals there is that which, if it stood at any moment visibly between us and the daily act of selfishness or injustice, would make us say with St Paul, *God forbid!* There is no unreality in seeing here the redemption of a world of sin through the unmerited sufferings of a minority; the unreal person is he who will not see it. Wherever we sit or stand or go, there is the 'fountain filled with blood' as truly as in any church; and there, as the author of *Piers Plowman* might have said with the change of three words 'Jesus Christ of Heaven in a dead soldier's semblance pursueth us ever.' 'Things and actions are what they are, and the consequences of them will be what they will be; why then, should we wish to be deceived?' Nothing but self-deception can blink the present redemption of the world through the soldier's sacrifice; and may we not say that it needs some dose of self-deception to ignore the explanation thus offered for the Christian's sense of redemption through Christ? Starting thus from generally acknowledged fact—starting from a point at which all can agree without effort or after-thought—we arrive almost necessarily at what I hope even the most religious persons will acknowledge to be a rudimentary Christianity. Let us for our part frankly confess to this qualification *rudimentary*; let us avow it to be a mere grain of mustard-seed as compared with the religion of the most religious persons. But it is a sound living grain, for what that is worth; and we all know what a grain of mustard-seed *may* be worth, if only men will give it a chance. If the man in the trenches could see plainly that all Christians had this microscopic modicum of living faith, and were ready to fraternize with him in virtue of that modicum which he himself possesses, then we should soon find ourselves in a new world.

But this needs give-and-take on both sides, not on one side only. We are inundated nowadays with pathetic protests that all present ideas of reconstruction are on wrong lines: that the world can be truly remodelled only if we envisage every problem and every man in the light of Christ. Very true; but why not begin at the other end also, and try to see Jesus Christ in every human being? That was the conscious motto of St Vincent de Paul, one of the greatest social reformers in all history, and one of the most irreproachably orthodox. If it be true that much of so-called progressive thought is an outrage upon Christ, it is still more true that we outrage him in the person of every fellow-man to whom we do injustice, not only actively, but even passively, by our conservative attachment to unjust traditions. The official church, like the man in the trenches, must give up certain false ideas and face certain more and more patent facts, before both can join together in the true spirit of Christ. We say to the unbeliever: 'If there were no more in the eucharist than this, that you cannot kneel there and think the thing over, even with only half

your mind, without feeling a little less uncharitable and
indifferent to the needs of others—if there were no more
than this, it would still be one of the most beneficent and
far-reaching institutions in the world.' But does not he
reply justly to us 'If you believe in the Christ of the
gospels, then you believe also in sweeping away every
convention that cannot justify itself under the search-
light of experience; and, to me, your worship of stale conventions poisons your very eucharist; when ye spread
forth your hands, your hands are full of blood; it was to
wash these things clean that my comrades gave their lives;
in those men's sacrifice, and not on the altar of your
churches, I see him that loved us, and hath made us kings
and priests unto God.'

At the present moment it needs some imagination to
grasp the reality of this religious cry from the trenches,
just as imagination is needed to realize No Man's Land or
a field-hospital. Yet in a few months, perhaps, the re-
turned soldier will be a concrete and visible person among
us; not one, but millions of them; are you then prepared
to hear Christ's voice in theirs when they speak in earnest,
just as we see Christ's blood in the blood of their dead companions? They will come back with a poignant sense of
reality which will go straight to thinking hearts; there will
be exaggeration, and revolt, and bitterness, in many of
their words; but something will come inexorably home to
us: we shall feel that the old state of things has been in
many ways reversed, and that we no longer look down
upon these men from a platform of privilege:

> 'Though I've belted you and flayed you,
> By the living God that made you
> You're a better man than I am, Gunga Dîn.

The collective force of that great multitude which no man
can number, who have passed through this great tribulation, will be the force of God's word, speaking through

human tongues and therefore requiring strict examination, but God's word in the main, and mainly to be understood through faith. Amid all this diversity of tongues, we shall doubtless find one or two ideas distinctly traceable; something like a clear and unanimous voice which will reason to us of righteousness and judgment to come; and we shall feel then, if not now already, that the parts have been reversed between us and them. It is no longer we who sit in judgment upon democracy after its appeal to Caesar: it is still, indeed, the common workman who stands at our bar; but he has now got hold of something we have hitherto failed to grasp, something of which we have now a dim inkling, yet which we still tremble to acknowledge in its entirety. We feel it a great venture of faith even to confess aloud: *Almost thou persuadest me.* And he makes answer: *I would to God that not only thou, but also all that hear me this day, were both almost and altogether such as I am, except these wounds.* If certain religious reforms were solemnly and unanimously recommended to the nation by all three estates of the realm, and both houses of convocation, and a conference of all the free churches, there would be no merit in accepting them. If, however, God suggests them to us only through people as insignificant individually as the Carpenter of Nazareth, does it not require some Christian faith to see what wheat there is here among the chaff?

For it is the paradox of all religious history that faith must always doubt of itself, or it is no true faith; the ancient truth can survive only on condition of becoming ever new; we are true to tradition only by breaking with tradition, since our own best traditions were born of a violent breach with the past. To worship God in spirit and in truth means the perpetual re-spiritualization of time-honoured truths. Just as we sit like Agrippa before Paul with his more and more inexorable insistence upon new and unwelcome truths....*Believest thou?—I know that thou believest*...so also we stand as the Jew did before the writer of the epistle to the Hebrews. Apart from the gospels, which must be the main theme of Christian study at all times, there can scarcely be a more timely book for us to read at this moment than that brief treatise, recording how a Jew, steeped in the scriptures and traditions of his race, found in those very scriptures and traditions the necessity for a freer, wider, higher faith. In detail, conservative theologians may find in it more support, perhaps, than in any other book of the Bible. But in spirit it is revolutionary, as showing how the conservatism of to-day is based upon a radical transmutation of religious values in the past: what is orthodox now was once violently destructive, in those days when it was a young and living faith. And, side by side with that book, may I recommend to all who have leisure and access to the university library one other brief book, and a third which is scarcely more than a pamphlet? You will find in Loisy's *L'Evangile et l'Eglise* (or in his *Autour d'un Petit Livre*, which is simply a defence of *L'Evangile et l'Eglise*) a very practical application of the spirit which inspired the writer to the Hebrews. And that which is put in an abstract form by Loisy is explained, by means of an imaginary concrete case, in Mr A. R. Waller's *Civilizing of the Matafanus*, a little book which is unfortunately, like Loisy's *L'Evangile et l'Eglise*, no longer in print. This pamphlet records the civilizing of an utterly barbarous race by a few apostles of higher culture, and shows most convincingly how truth can be brought home to unprepared minds only by perpetual compromise, which again involves perpetual restatements and readjustments, since at each forward step the hearer is not only ready for fresh truth, but imperatively needs such renovation in order to keep that mental balance without which no effective grasp of truth is possible[81].

I have already apologized for the necessarily discursive character of these lectures: but you will, I hope, have found them consistent all through in their plea for immediate reform, as the only alternative to ultimate, and possibly not far distant, revolution. We are perhaps unduly inclined to pity and excuse those majorities who, in times of revolution, groan under the excesses of wild minorities. We say of the Russians: 'These people asked only to be left in quiet: yet the Tsarist oppressed them yesterday, and the Bolshevik to-day.' But what right had they, after all, to ask only for quiet? If majorities refuse to look into the future, and to face the changes for which present facts are clamouring day by day, and to stake something upon those changes—as even the most careful investor must risk something unless he puts his money away in an old stocking—then they have partly themselves to thank when they find themselves over-ridden roughshod by a noisy minority, which has at least the virtue of superior courage. It may be impossible to decide whether Tsarist or Bolshevik bears the heavier responsibility for the present sufferings of Russia: but it cannot be doubted that, if the mass of the population could have shown more political sense and initiative, despotism might have been abolished without the alternative plague of anarchy. May we not apply this lesson directly to the problem of religious reform? Here also the majority would probably be puzzled to choose between two unreasonable extremes. It is quite arguable that the flat atheist dishonours God one degree less than the other extremist who preaches his own personal absurdities, or the exploded absurdities of his clique, as God's immutable word. Plutarch commands our sympathy in expressing a preference for the man who should deny that there was any such person as Plutarch over another who might credit Plutarch with his own follies and vices. We may hesitate, then, in clearly assigning the bad preëminence to either extremist; but we can scarcely deny that it will be our own fault if we fall into the hands of either. Nevertheless, one or other extremist will cer-

tainly control the situation, unless we control it ourselves
For each of these men satisfies, in an exaggerated form, a
real human need. Unless we anticipate to some considerable extent the atheist's spirit of adventure, and the
traditionalist's regard for the past, a dissatisfied world will
always be capable of rushing into one of those two exaggerations. And (though a man is always prone to extol his
own personal interests) I have tried all through to suggest
that the spirit of real reform, the spirit that seeks by its
moderation to disarm both the religious Tsarist and the
religious Bolshevik, will necessarily lay great stress on the
historical side of the question. We are threatened at
present by those who, even if their doctrines be otherwise
true, seem to introduce a fatal confusion by substituting
false historical claims for the stronger, though less tangible,
moral claim. On the other hand, the reaction from these
false claims may lead to the no less fatal error of those who,
in their impatience, attempt to make a clean sweep of the
past. We need to remember what Jakob Grimm said to
the extremists in the Frankfort Parliament of 1848: 'A
party that wants to have no past, will have no future.'
The philosophical differences between rival schools of religious belief and unbelief might be adjusted, if once we
could come to some rough agreement about the historical
facts.

    And this is why I have tried to emphasize the Franciscan
parallel. We have here a splendid field for study in what
an Italian professor has called religious embryology.
Having already indicated this in detail, I will conclude
here with some more general considerations.

    The Franciscan student soon finds that there were two
men in St Francis, and two religions in his message.
I know no single anecdote which brings this out so well as
one which I have already quoted elsewhere; one of his
humbler companions tells the tale. 'The Holy Master was
wont to leave his cell about the third hour [9 a.m.]; and,

if he saw no fire in the kitchen, he would go down into the garden and pluck a handful of herbs which he brought home, saying: "Cook these, and it will be well with the brethren." And, whereas at times I was wont to set before him eggs and milk food which the faithful had sent us, with some sort of gravy stew, then he would eat cheerfully with the rest and say, "Thou hast done too much, brother; I will that thou prepare naught for the morrow, nor do aught in my kitchen." So I, following his precepts absolutely and in all points, cared for nothing so much as to obey that most holy man; when therefore he came, and saw the table laid with divers crusts of bread, he would begin to eat gaily thereof, but presently he would chide me that I brought no more, asking me why I had cooked naught. Whereunto I answered, "For that thou, Father, badest me cook none." But he would say, "Dear son, discretion is a noble virtue; nor shouldst thou always fulfil all that thy superior biddeth thee, especially when he is troubled by any passion*."' The very human element in this story makes the saint all the more real and lovable to us; but it explains why even before his death there were irreconcilable parties in his order. In his immediate *entourage* things went well enough as a rule; the saint was always there to be consulted, and the divine common-sense which underlay all his divine enthusiasm made him a clear and trusted oracle  But, when the order had outgrown this stage, and when there were thousands who had scarcely set eyes upon the Founder, this great body needed clear principles; and it became evident that St Francis had always oscillated between two ultimately irreconcilable principles. Any real breach with the Roman church was unthinkable to him; Rome never had a more loyal son, in all intention, than he. On the other hand, the things that made his real originality were quite irreconcilable with the practice, or even the principles, of the official Roman

* Wadding, *Annales Minorum*, anno 1258.

church, such as it was then or as it has been at any time
since. We have only to think of a single point; the rule of
absolute poverty; 'we expressly forbid that any man touch
money: whether directly or *per interpositam personam.*'
If that single rule became canon law and papal practice
how long could the Catholic church last in anything like
its present form? Not, of course, that St Francis ever prescribed this regulation for the whole church; but such an
extension is none the less logically implied in his mission.
It was of the essence of his doctrine that the evangelical
life *par excellence* necessarily involved this attitude of re-
pulsion towards money; one of the Franciscan tenets was
this, that Christ and his apostles had been not only individually but corporately poor. From this it followed
that the hierarchy was making no attempt to live the strict
evangelical life; and this consequence was none the less
inevitable because St Francis himself studiously avoided
facing it. This it was which brought the spiritual Franciscans finally into conflict with the official church; until
men were burned for holding doctrines that had been
implicit in the Founder's words, and explicitly defended
in the early days by even a moderate like St Bonaventura.

So it was also with Christ. This is most clearly put, perhaps, by Auguste Sabatier in his *Esquisse d'une Philosophie
de la Religion*[82]. 'Jesus,' writes Sabatier, 'chose to abolish
nothing [of the Jewish law] authoritatively: he preferred to
confirm the whole tradition, claiming to inherit and not to
destroy it (Matt. v. 17): "Think not that I am come to
destroy the law or the Prophets; I am not come to destroy,
but to fulfil." His method is the method of the sower, to
whom he so loves to compare himself. In the furrow
ploughed by his word through the old soil of Judaism, he
dropped quietly and noiselessly a new seed...nothing was
less violent; but nothing could be more fundamentally
revolutionary, because nothing could be more fertile than
this.... We can see very clearly the inevitable consequences

of this method, because we can trace them historically; but those who listened to Christ's words could not see. They never suspected that a day would come when they must say farewell to Moses in loyalty to their Master; who, on the whole, had submitted to the law all through, and had been (as St Paul calls him) "a minister of circumcision" (Rom. xv. 8). On the morrow of his death, his disciples were far from any breach with Judaism.... This took more than a century of controversy and strife.'

Strife and controversy, yes; but life and progress all the while: a firm hand on the present, and a firm face set towards the future. The Bible, which is so often treated as a refuge for conservatism, is essentially a revolutionary book.... 'Old things are passed away; behold, all things are become new' (2 Cor. v. 17).... 'Forgetting those things which are behind, and reaching forth unto those things which are before, I press toward the mark for the prize of the high calling of God in Christ Jesus' (Phil. iii. 13, 14). Running thus, we have Christ by our side, and the great cloud of witnesses around us. It is the one living way, the one way of losing our life that we may find it. Moreover, it is not only the way of religion, but that of philosophy also. Socrates went that way. Against the arguments of the sophists, which would have led the world to universal scepticism, he set up no vain barriers of tradition, but came down to meet the sceptics on their own ground. He rejected as frankly as they the fables that merely dishonoured the gods; admitted just as frankly that our senses may be, and frequently are, deceived at every point; and then showed how, behind and above the fallible particular, stands the universal, externally true and to some extent knowable by all who will truly seek. Whether we hear or whether we forbear—however much we may choose to deceive ourselves—the fact will still remain that mere passive acquiescence never has worked for the redemption of humanity; that always, even among the traditionalists, those whose faith is strong and living have had to buy it with just as many struggles as the revolutionaries; and that now, as always, every human being must in the last resort answer individually, in his own mind, that question which God will not and man cannot decide for us—'Am I indeed following after him that should come, or do I look for another?'

# EPILOGUE

THE lectures were followed by an hour of discussion. I am grateful to the critics whose objections have compelled me to clarify my meaning in text or notes, and to add an appendix dealing with two fundamental points. But, on the whole, the discussion strengthened my conviction that, side by side with many differences which may be inevitable, there are many others which ought no longer to divide the followers of Christ. Nothing was brought forward which radically affected the following fundamental propositions.

(1) Many things now taught as essential by the clergy are primarily questions of historical fact, and therefore pertain less to the theologian's province than to that of the historian.

(2) Under closer examination, these so-called historical essentials are found to lack much of the double character claimed for them. From the *historical* point of view, specialists are increasingly unwilling to dogmatize, and there is probably no historian of eminence who would now defend that cruder theory of apostolical succession which was popular a generation ago, and is still frequently propounded by theologians[83]. Conservative writers commonly content themselves now with the far simpler task of combating liberal exaggerations[84]. Again, as to *essentials*, we find that great saints have taught a doctrine of miracles which permits immense latitude of belief.

(3) There are, admittedly, very serious gaps in our historical evidence of the earliest Christian origins; and these can only be filled by inference or by imagination. In the Franciscan movement, which is probably the nearest historical parallel to the apostolic age, such inferences are

demonstrably very dangerous; and a closer study of Franciscan origins makes it far more difficult to dogmatize about apostolic origins.

(4) Meanwhile, the insistence upon these points as historical facts, and as essentials of any religious concordat, does in fact alienate thousands who would have done credit to the church alike from the intellectual and from the moral point of view.

(5) Lastly, it is increasingly rare for the most thoughtful young men to commit themselves, by ordination, to a lifelong support of the current doctrines.

If these five points are granted—and there seemed no serious disposition to dispute them—it would appear to follow that some real change of heart is needed. It is preeminently the exclusivist spirit within the church which is on its trial; it seems suicidal for the clergy to preach separation on the strength of unproved theories. Apart from the true vine, Christianity will doubtless wither; but no less fatal must be its separation from the common soil of human society. The clergy must reconsider their attitude towards those thousands who are really religious but not orthodox; it is from the clergy that this present crisis demands the greatest venture of faith.

In Newman's famous parallel between Roman catholicism and early Christianity, there is one high quality which he does not, because he cannot, claim for the church of his own day[85]. The priest is no longer the zealous and irrepressible missionary, wearing his heart on his sleeve. If he saw a fellow-traveller reading the Bible, he would think it impertinent to strike in with an 'understandest thou what thou readest?' (Acts viii. 30) The educated laity, on the other hand, often feel that they are taking an unfair advantage of a priest by leading him into religious discussion. The church no longer attacks, but digs herself in; the fear of losing belief by free interchange of thought seems to outweigh the hope of kindling faith in others. Yet how seldom, in the Bible, are *faith* and *belief* used for attachment to past things, in comparison with their use for present guidance or future hopes[86]! Those who entrench themselves for faith's sake have lost the salt of faith already. The church must come out into the open again, not occasionally but habitually; only so can she fulfil her divine mission. It is not enough that her gold was once tried seven times in the furnace; with every generation there must be a fresh purging of the dross. She cannot possibly lose, in the long run, by the appeal to history, or by the most naked exposition of her credentials side by side with those of the agnostic.

History shows us both man's littleness and his greatness, teaching us infinite patience and infinite hope. The spirit seems to move almost blindly upon the face of the waters from age to age; mankind staggers on from failure to failure; the heart is sick with hope deferred; insuccess begins to look like a fatal law of nature. Then, suddenly, in the twinkling of an eye, comes a new world; yet not so, even then, but that many will be blind to it, and many will blaspheme. But faith looks beyond these uncertainties, and marks how, while each individual effort is infinitely small, the sum of separate energies is infinitely great. *De minimis non curat lex; de minimis aedificatur ecclesia Dei;* 'he that contemneth small things shall fall by little and little' (Ecclus. xix. 1).

By little and little the institutional churches have lost ground during the past few generations. Yet the world outside grows in hope; never has it seemed more living than it seems to the average man of to-day. That long nightmare of world-senility and imminent doom which haunted the middle ages is dispelled; it is only as fossils that such phrases survive as 'The world is very evil, the times are waxing late.' The average churchman shares the general optimism; just as the outsider feels himself less godless than by law he ought to be, so the orthodox hopes the same on his account. *The Church in the Furnace* is only one of a dozen books in which this hope may be read; the war has hastened many possibilities of reconciliation that had long been growing[87]. 'There is a great tide running in the hearts of men. The hearts of men have never beaten so singularly in unison before. Men have never before been so conscious of their brotherhood[88].' Is not this, then, the accepted time for a frank recognition of the fact that nothing in Christianity can outweigh the honest desire to follow Christ? Without prejudice to those individual convictions which perhaps can never come to mutual reconciliation, may not we find some public and regular acknowledgment of our general unity in Christ?

Every delay adds to the difficulty of the task. Indoors and out, in fireside talk or railway-train discussions, we find men beginning to speak of the official churches as Tertullian's Christian spoke of the age-long traditions of heathendom: 'We are men of yesterday, but we have struck root everywhere among you; we permeate your cities and villages, your councils, your camps, your markets; it is only in your temples that we leave you to yourselves[89].' The churchman's answer now is too often what the pagan's answer then was; a boast of past glories and greatness. In his self-concentration, he too often ignores the real forces which are arrayed against him. However it may have been at any other time, this opposition is no longer governed mainly by self-assertion, self-conceit, or the spirit of mere denial. The serious adversary of to-day is not the atheist; Hyde Park orators do not find their audiences increase in proportion as church congregations dwindle. Men are crying for a God which the churches too seldom give them; it is the moderates who are drifting away; the dissidents are often typified in our wounded officers—brave, patient and modest. They know what they lose by religious isolation; they reckon their loss more exactly, perhaps, than some of those to whom gregarious religion comes so easily. Those of them who do fall into line, are apt to wonder whether they have not bought fellowship at too dear a price. Yet they know the real value of such fellowship; they still see in Christendom the greatest and purest aggregate of men and women publicly professing a common ideal. The average or weaker mind is as ready to recognize a protecting church as the sick man is to cry aloud for his mother. Stronger and more stubborn souls, again, are often quick to acknowledge other greatnesses; they are even glad, for once, to put off the burden of their own masterfulness: 'Ô seigneur, j'ai vécu puissant et solitaire[90]!' But the church casts away all these advantages when she erects artificial barriers between religious emotion and intellectual life. The minds thus alienated are lost for ever; time only hardens them in their repugnance to a creed whose plenipotentiaries demand this unreasonable sacrifice of reason. Many of them have read widely enough to contrast the almost hysterical dogmatism of a large proportion of the priesthood with the almost agnostic caution of real scholars among the priestly party; and the conviction grows upon them that, outside the institutional churches, there is a church of truth which the priest does not recognize. We forbid to these men all fellowship with the saints of the calendar; and they turn away to the saints of science with an ardour which may be partly negative and rebellious, but which is certainly due in part to a just sense of indignation. 'We leave you now' (they say) 'to your temples; we leave you all the externals of what has been the greatest of all visible spiritual heritages; for ourselves, we ask nothing but the inward conviction that we have broken only with the letter of the past, and that the eternal spirit is even more truly with us than with you. Without presuming to judge others in their conformity, we find in our own conscience that which would make further acquiescence a treason. If indeed it be no more possible for you to concede one inch of your religious heritage or your religious intuitions than it is for us to smother the voice of our intellectual conscience, then it seems plain that God must intend further divisions among those who follow him; for we are ready to believe that the contrary convictions of others may be as genuine and legitimate as our own. Yet we can never test such divergent convictions too often or too impartially; therefore, before you and we have drifted altogether out of hearing, we may justly appeal once more with that most searching question of all: "Are you assured of Christ's inspiration when you command us, on the very threshold of your church, to accept as certain the things that are yet unproved?"'

# APPENDIX

TWO questions raised in discussion by members of my audience are so fundamental that they require separate treatment here.

(A) My definition of *Christian* on p. 17 was disputed. Some hearers contended that the belief in Christ's divinity is an essential part of Christianity, and that no creed lacking this belief could truly be called Christian[1]; it was claimed that the belief in Christ as God is already recorded in the Epistle to the Hebrews, and has never ceased to be of the essence of Christianity.

This contention involves one obvious difficulty on the very threshold. It is certainly usual to reckon modern Unitarians among Christian bodies; and it is common also to apply the term to the ancient Ebionites and Arians, who denied or doubted the absolute divinity of Christ. Nor is this merely a loose way of speaking; for in Canon Law these two latter are reckoned, not among pagans or Jews, but among heretics, though the Ebionites are called *semi-judaei* (Gratian, *Decret.* pars II, Causa XXIV. q. 3). Indeed, the official church herself has shown the greatest reluctance to clear away loose ideas on this subject by exact definition. The *Catholic Dictionary* says (3rd ed. p. 158): 'Probably the heathen at Antioch mistook *Christus* for a proper name, and called the disciples *Christiani* just as they called those who adhered to Pompey's party *Pompeiani*....In later times the word has been used (1) for those who imitate the life as well as hold the faith of Christ, (2) for Catholics, (3) for baptized persons who believe in Christ, (4) for all baptized persons.' Aquinas in one place solemnly adopts

[1] Or, as one of them modified it, 'no creed lacking the belief that *either* Christ is God *or*, at any rate, that those who believe Christ to be God have a true conception of God.'

the first of these definitions, in a form which would exclude our calling even the Pope a Christian, unless his personal life were such that he could truly be said to 'have crucified the flesh, with the affections and lusts thereof' (2ª 2ᵃᵉ, Quaest. cxxiv. art. 5, m. 1). But in his discussion of the distinction between heresy, Judaism, and paganism, he distinctly implies adherence to the last and most usual definition, that all baptized are Christians (2ª 2ᵃᵉ, Quaest. x., xi.). Therefore, in the absence of official definition for this term, which the church must long ago have defined quite clearly if she had felt sufficiently sure of herself, we are compelled to fall back upon the evidence of history. To whom has the name in fact been applied?

Even if we admit that the writer to the Hebrews asserts the divinity of Christ in anything like the Nicene sense (which would be disputed by perhaps the majority of Bible students), how far does this take us back? At the very earliest, to 63 A.D.; and a good many scholars would put it later. This still leaves a gap of thirty years, during which the doctrine may well have gone through changes as revolutionary as we have noted among the early Franciscans, not only on the subject of book-learning, but even in their central doctrine of poverty. Therefore, though my critics have a right to believe that the thoughts of 63 A.D. were also the thoughts of 33 A.D., it would seem impossible to claim strictly historical evidence, in the ordinary sense of the words, for this belief. Moreover, there are many expressions in other N.T. books which, so far from supporting the strict Nicene doctrine, are very difficult to reconcile with it.

Taking the plain facts admitted in the *Catholic Dictionary*, and considering them as objectively as we should consider the rise of the Bábí religion, must we not admit that they seem to favour the broadest possible definition? They imply (1) that the name, when first used, was a parallel formation to *Pompeian* (or, as I have put it in my text, to *Gladstonian*); (2) that, if belief in anything like the Nicene conception had been held essential from the first, it must have been thus defined unambiguously at a very early stage; and (3) that the four quite irreconcilable definitions now current (to which we must add my critics' as a fifth) supply a pretty clear proof of the uncertainty of the church herself as to who is a Christian, and who an outsider. Therefore I should answer my critics still, as I answered them in the lecture room, that their words contained a quite correct *description* of what is in the minds of the majority (though perhaps no great majority) of *modern* Christians; but that history alone can decide whether that would have been the *definition* of those who had most right to define—Christ himself or his immediate disciples. In other words, their conviction is very legitimate as a personal opinion; but it would be quite illegitimate to build upon it as an ascertained fact.

(B)    Another critic found serious fault with my analogy of the 'religious capitalist' (p. 7), objecting:

'If truth is the most precious thing in the world, how have we the right to forgo it even for the sake of charity and unity? How can the catholic Christian, who honestly believes that our Lord was not only Perfect Man but also Incarnate God—a belief that is interwoven with his whole being, which he holds both intellectually and experientially, and which is fortified by the reasoning and experience of others all down the centuries—give up that truth to meet the agnostic "poor man"? The truth is not his to surrender. Nor would it be a true sacrifice for the sake of others, as the economic one would be; the catholic renunciation would not enrich the agnostic.'

This is in fact an objection which I had anticipated. The reader may see how I pleaded that the concession need only be '*ad interim*' (p. 7): that the question is, not whether the catholic can *give up* certain beliefs, but whether he can treat them as 'non-essential' (p. 8) ; that his concession need only amount to 'a suspension of judgment' (p. 58) in order that Christianity might become again (as I believe it to have been originally) a creed which allowed 'the greatest possible liberty for divergent conceptions.' Finally, in Lecture VII, I stated in brief the whole gist of this present objection, and attempted to meet it (pp. 123–5). But my critic is still convinced that to plead for such a temporary suspension of judgment as would compel the catholic to fraternize with people of divergent conceptions, is equivalent to asking him to abandon the truth for the sake of other people's ideas. I must therefore attempt to meet this objection more fully.

(1) I maintain that the analogy of my text (pp. 7–8) is far closer than my critic seems willing to allow. The religious capitalist is not asked to give up his capital, but to put himself in a position which would enable the religious pauper to reap more advantage from this capital, so far as circumstances allow. My suggestion is analogous, not to such a renunciation of property as that of St Francis, but to the action of a rich landowner who shares his park with the public, at the risk of some accidental or even mischievous damage. My whole contention is that the present attitude of the church gives the majority of our population very little chance of conversion to Christianity. A catholic naturally finds it difficult to agree with this; but it is necessary for the comprehension of these lectures to realize that this is my starting-point, that the proportion of non-Christian households is rapidly increasing, and that the insistence on separatist doctrines as fundamental signifies the growth of an enormous population which has no chance of hearing Christ simply preached. Moreover, this is strongly borne out by the evidence of irreproachably orthodox chaplains: see notes 5 and 6. From this starting-point, the natural inference is that something must at last

be done to simplify Christ's message for the average man; and therefore that such concessions as I suggest would in fact 'enrich the agnostic' in a considerable number of cases. Many honest agnostics have never yet had a chance of understanding Christianity. However we ourselves may choose to ignore this, our children will freely confess it.

(2) Far more serious is the objection that the catholic cannot abandon his present position without giving away a truth which is not his to give. This objection involves not only historical but also psychological considerations; and the latter may conveniently be taken first.

(a) My critic claims intuitive and subjective force for his convictions; they rest not only on an *intellectual* but also on an *experiential* basis. I have tried elsewhere to make it quite clear that I contest no man's right to hold such convictions; that, on the contrary, I believe certain things to be apprehended only by faith, and that I have nothing but respectful admiration for every real venture of faith. If, after stating this in so many words on p. 103, I seem afterwards to show scant sympathy with certain ventures of faith in other directions, this is only because I doubt (and supply reasons for my doubt) whether the real faith is not there mixed with much fundamental un-faith. This, however, is a matter in which no man can definitely judge another; he can only state his suspicions plainly, and ask the other to reflect very seriously whether he clings to his present belief because it is the highest possible, or only because other alternatives seem, at first sight, too cruel to be faced.

Motives are always mixed; we cling to a faith, as to a parent, not only because of its intrinsic virtues but also because it is our own. These elements may be combined in infinitely variable proportions, from the man whose faith is almost free from egoism, down to the man who has scarcely any reason for belief beyond passive conservatism or personal caprice. And, quite apart from the shifting

APPENDIX 167

proportions of these two elements, which we may call variations in *purity*, beliefs may also vary almost infinitely in *intensity*. We have therefore to judge a creed by two factors, its intensity and its purity, which are by no means always proportional to each other; so that the more luke-warm creed may be redeemed by its superior purity, or the more mixed creed by its superior intensity. This complicates our task; but such complications are the very salt of life; it is by confronting us with such problems that God proves us from day to day. We may passionately admire a man's faith, yet no less passionately desire that something should be changed in it; we may obstinately refuse to accept its quality even while we covet its intensity.

The analogy of filial love, already hinted at, may help us here. Children love more or less purely, more or less intensely. We admire a girl's devotion to her mother, and we take it for granted that she thinks her mother the best in the world. But we desire this to be a positive faith in the parent's actual virtues, not an egoistic and negative faith involving depreciation of other women—'*my* mother, right or wrong!' Yet even in this latter case, in spite of the baser negative alloy, we may be inspired by the intensity of the girl's faith, and wish nothing changed in her but her exclusivism. We feel that such a girl would not really love her own mother less for allowing a little more good in other people's mothers. She herself may feel that she would; but the outsider's conviction is that she is mentally confusing the pure and essential elements of her love with other personal, and even anti-social, elements.

Is it not thus in religion also? Newman's faith was splendid in its intensity; but there was a strong negative element in it. To keep his faith, he turned deliberately away from much that has been most fertile in modern thought, and rejected things from which the world will never now go back. We admire his conviction; we say: 'A thousand times better such faith than no faith at all!' But may we not desire that this faith should have rested on a broader basis, even though it had thus lost somewhat in intensity? That my Anglo-catholic critic, after suspending judgment for awhile to consider opposing beliefs more sympathetically, would find some change in his own creed, is quite possible. Indeed, I from my side am bound to believe in this as more than possible; nor is it right for me to disguise this belief, so long as I do not attempt to prejudge the main issue by basing any argument upon what, after all, is only a private belief of my own. But is it not equally probable that, even supposing the creed thus to lose in intensity, it would gain still more in purity by the elimination of its predominantly negative elements?

Moreover, can we take it for granted that it would lose even in intensity? May we not find room here for the paradox noted by Bishop Butler, that in proportion as a sick-nurse gains experience, while her merely instinctive horror of suffering diminishes, she becomes all the more resourceful in her fight against human suffering? Is not the apparent intensity of filial love sometimes due to the contrast between the child's affection for the parent and its indifference to outsiders? And may not religious exclusiveness sometimes give an exaggerated impression of positive faith through the heightened colour which it takes from its negative qualities?

We are convinced that $2 \times 2 = 4$. To study mathematics for a short time under consideration of the contrary proposition that $2 \times 2 = 5$ might conceivably involve some transitory weakening of our belief in the multiplication table. But, in this case, the serious consideration of contrary theories would leave us finally under a still firmer conviction that $2 \times 2 = 4$. If present society were seriously divided into two classes, those who believed $2 \times 2 = 4$ and others who claimed that $2 \times 2 = 5$, and if the cleavage threatened to become daily deeper and more disastrous, should we not roughly measure the faith of the former class by their willingness to give the contrary theory a trial, and by their conviction that such a trial would gain for their party far more converts than they could possibly lose in perverts? The foregoing considerations may help to clear our minds; but there is a point at which purely psychological arguments become irrelevant to this question. A catholic may assert not only his subjective and experiential conviction, but also his intuitive feeling that any serious and sympathetic consideration of contrary convictions, and any attempt to put himself at the doubter's point of view, is treason to God and to the truth. In other words, he claims to rest altogether on intuition; and no man has a philosophical right to deny another's claims to intuition.

(b) Here, then, comes the historical argument, which amounts to an appeal from the dubieties of speculation to the clearer test of practice. We cannot lay too great emphasis on Christ's criterion, 'by their fruits ye shall know them,' so long as we always try to survey the whole ground, not arguing from isolated cases but seeking the widest available generalizations.

Bossuet and Leibnitz were divided by exactly the same philosophical gulf which has been indicated above. To Bossuet's pathetic plea 'permettez-moy encore de vous prier, en finissant, d'examiner sérieusement devant Dieu si vous avez quelque bon moyen d'empescher l'Église de devenir éternellement variable en présupposant qu'elle peut errer et changer ses décrets sur la foy,' Leibnitz replied 'il nous plaist, Monseigneur, d'estre de cette Église tousjours mouvante et éternellement variable.' Bossuet could not remain an orthodox Roman catholic and admit even the possibility of a single error in the decrees of the council of Trent. Leibnitz took a view irreconcilable with this; the philosophical deadlock was hopeless, and further discussion became possible only when the venue was changed to historical ground. There, Leibnitz proved the errors of the council of Trent in the matter of the Biblical canon by such overwhelming documentary evidence that Bossuet was reduced to silence. And we, who have also the evidence of those four generations which have elapsed since Bossuet wrote, can appeal still more directly to history to judge the great bishop's arguments. He found it impossible to meet Leibnitz on common ground. Intellectually and experientially, he was convinced that any such concession would be treason to God and to the truth. How does history judge this attitude? How many, among Roman catholics themselves, would seriously argue in these days that it is impossible, even provisionally, to get behind the decrees of Trent? The Creed of Pius IV binds them nominally to Bossuet's position; but do they in fact take their creed much more seriously here than in that other obligation which it lays upon them to promote the slaying of heretics? (see note 66). And what is the present ecclesiastical state of Bossuet's France, the Eldest Daughter of the Church? It is almost impossible for a French socialist to be a practising Christian. Even the recent reaction in favour of catholicism, limited as it is, is to a great extent not religious but political; it is notorious that men like Maurice Barrès are not believers in any vital sense, but simply anti-anticlericals, who would hold a brief for Mahomadanism if Mahomadanism supported their social and political theories. Even if we assume the present religious state of Germany to be still less definitely Christian than that of France, we gain nothing here. Bossuet feared lest concession on his part would spell ruin to the Christian religion. He stood immovably on this ground, concession was ruled out as unthinkable, and the result is that, according to Dr Figgis, we no longer live in a Christian world. Leibnitz, on the other hand, was convinced that, if Christians could manage to present a united front, their cause would gain immensely: do not the events of the last 120 years rather favour than contradict this view?

For it cannot too often be repeated that my plea is not for the obliteration of differences between Christians, but only for the recognition of the secondary importance of such differences, as compared with the one central fact that all Christians are trying to follow Christ. Another critic of my lectures asked me how the proposed concordat of different denominations would differ from unitarianism, and why, therefore, it should be expected to succeed better than unitarianism has succeeded. My reply was obvious; unitarianism is a single limb; my contention is that all the limbs should do what they can to form a single body, not by artificial conjunction, but by coveting each for himself, and striving to share with each other, the one spirit which must govern all who try honestly to follow Christ. Such a body might never become a political unity, perhaps; but at least it would preserve spiritual unity: let us have a living Christian federation, if not a single Christian state. Such a confederation would add to the virtues of the catholic those of the unitarian also; for I should hold it waste of time to argue with objectors who deny any virtue whatever to unitarianism. The world as it is, is confessedly slipping away from Christianity; and exclusivist theories, where they are not demonstrably unhistorical, are so vague as to give us no real help. From this I conclude that, if we could recognize such vagueness (with some amount of consequent friction) as a part of Christ's heritage to his church, we should then accept this as an inevitable element in our present life of probation. Thus we should put out at last upon the unknown ocean of completest possible toleration, not only because Christ himself ventured so much for the sake of inclusion; not only because the whole trend of civilization has been towards the successive removal of mental and spiritual barriers once deemed insuperable; but, even more, because these vast waters seem to be the only religious sea yet unexplored, while all other coasts are littered with the wrecks of Christian faith.

# NOTES

1, p. 3. It is difficult otherwise to explain the facts that the English mystics all hail from the eastern counties or the eastern midlands, and that these districts, with London, were the predominantly Lollard districts. The ideas which gave the impetus to this movement would naturally follow the great trade routes; we know how they spread from the Upper to the Lower Rhine, and the germs (to keep up the metaphor of the text) would naturally be carried to those parts of England which were most accessible to Rhenish trade. It is true that the Lollard writings contain little or no mysticism in the strict sense; but it has long since been noted that a wave of mysticism always brings with it a wave of free-thought; it begins with independent soul-working within orthodox limitations, but spreads in many cases, by an almost inevitable impulse, beyond those limitations. My authority for a good deal of what is asserted on pp. 2–4 is an author who would doubtless have dissented from some of my deductions—the late Father Denifle, in *Archiv für Litteratur- und Kirchengeschichte des M. A.* vol. II. pp. 417 ff.

But I must here guard against certain misconceptions to which (as I now find) my necessarily concise language has given rise.

(1) There is no *absolute* distinction between scholasticism and mysticism; between what one of my audience called '*intellectual* truth and *mystical* truth.' On the contrary (a) scholasticism was inspired by mystical devotion, and (b) mysticism seldom freed itself entirely from scholastic elements in the middle ages. As Denifle puts it, 'mysticism is not really, as people so often assert, the antithesis of scholasticism' (p. 426).

(2) The 'teaching' of the nuns by these *docti fratres* would be mainly through sermons and the ordinary channels of spiritual direction; it was not 'teaching' in an academic sense.

(3) By 'the *language* of the intellect, etc.' I did not for a moment intend to imply that Latin is not the language of the heart as well as of the intellect. I used *language* in its frequent sense of *phraseology*; scholastic formularies had to be translated, to some considerable extent, into the simpler and more meta-phorical phraseology of intuition. This would modify the teacher's thought even more than the simultaneous process of translating from Latin to German.

(4) I have insufficiently guarded myself in the text against the natural misconception that I meant to assert a *direct* connexion between the thought of the Rhenish mystics and Juliana, and from

her to Margery Backster. Yet my sentence, even in its original cruder form, did not involve any assertion of identity of doctrine among the persons named, but only of stimulus by contagion. We may illustrate this by a conspicuous modern example. Newman, who ended in the Roman Church, was much influenced by the low-church Thomas Scott and by the somewhat latitudinarian Whately; and, again, the theory of evolution in church history which did so much to reconcile Newman to Romanism has been bound up, in Loisy, with theories which have taken him out of the church. Bolshevism (to take another example) is giving birth to, or at least stimulating, ideas which can hardly be reconciled with original Bolshevik principles. Every movement of thought produces reactions and cross-currents, sometimes in very unexpected directions; I noted this some years ago in *From St Francis to Dante* (2nd ed. p. 164) and summarized it so briefly in the present text as to become obscure. Nobody would assert that mysticism, by itself, could have produced the reformation of the sixteenth century; but it seems difficult to deny that it was one of the many currents which led to that great revolution.

**2**, p. 6. J. N. Figgis, *Civilisation at the Cross-Roads*, 1912, pp. 10, 24. Cf. the two following extracts from two distinguished chaplains at the front, in *The Church in the Furnace* (Macmillan, 1918). Canon F. B. Macnutt writes on pp. 14, 15: 'Why are the vast majority of the men who compose our armies almost completely unconscious of any sense of fellowship with the Church of their Baptism? Why is the religion of most soldiers so largely inarticulate that, as Donald Hankey has told us in *A Student in Arms*, they fail to connect the good things which they do believe and practise in any way with Jesus Christ? Why have they cast off what early teaching they had like garments which do not fit them and for which they have no use?...There is a remarkable consensus of judgment among those who are most capable to speak.' And the Rev. E. Milner-White, Fellow of King's College, Cambridge, says plainly on pp. 184, 194: 'Hardly a soldier carries a Prayer-book, because there is little in it he can use....Past stoic endurance of unintelligible collects has led the men's minds to expect no reality or meaning in the "prayer" part of the service [at the front].'

**3**, p. 7. *Piers Plowman*, B. XI. pp. 179 ff.

**4**, pp. 8, 17. These paragraphs are discussed at greater length in the Appendix.

**5**, p. 8. J. N. Figgis, *Civilisation at the Cross-Roads*, 1912, pp. 29 –35. 'Does there seem much more ground for saying that we live in a Christian world, beyond what might have been said in the

time of Tertullian, 200 A.D.? In many ways, there is less ground.
...Would there be a very large proportion of Christians at any
meeting of scholars or scientific men? Is there, in any real sense,
at the Universities?...The intellectual atmosphere we breathe is
no longer Christian.' Compare this with further testimony from
*The Church in the Furnace*. Canon F. B. Macnutt writes (p. 25) :
'The cause of Christ hangs in the balance, the issues are joined.
We know that for the Church, as far as we are concerned, it is now
or never.' The Rev. F. R. Barry, Fellow of Oriel College, Oxford,
speaks equally plainly on pp. 41, 47 and 67 : 'Many of your
cherished, untried faiths (in the sense of beliefs) may very likely
have to be surrendered. Traditional Christianity, I fancy, seems
to most men more remote than ever from the actual concerns of
life....The Church has specialised in irrelevancies, and she will
never grip the age with these. It is an age that is hungering for
reality....(p. 62) : One often feels that conventional Christianity
contains very little that is distinctively Christian....Hence comes
the paralysing unreality of the orthodox presentation of the
Christ....Traditional Christianity is on its trial. The next few
years, I believe, will give the decision whether it will or will not
be the world's religion. More and more men are turning away un-
satisfied from what we have been accustomed to set before them.'
    The Rev. E. S. Woods, Examining Chaplain to the Bishop of
Durham, is equally emphatic: 'A third essential and immediate
duty is that of *restating the Christian message* in thought and language that the ordinary man of to-day can understand. There
are multitudes of men and women who long to hear of God and
Christ, but are wearied and disgusted with the conventional and
ecclesiastical shibboleths that are too often offered them instead.
...For indeed, for the Church of England, it is now or never. It
is not conceivable that the voice of God could sound for her with
more trumpet-like clearness than it does to-day' (pp. 448–9).

    **6**, p. 9. See H. G. Wells, *God the Invisible King*, 1918, and the
following extract selected by a reviewer from Dr Benjamin Kidd's
posthumous volume (*The Science of Power*, 1918). 'The master
fact of the social integration is that the science of power in civilization is the science of the passion of the ideal. The passion of the
ideal is the passion of perfection, which is the passion for God.'
Here, again, is the testimony of a chaplain from the front: 'In
close connection with his lack of education in religious matters is
the soldier's attitude towards God. He does believe in the existence
of God....But his belief in God is in a state of arrested development. It might almost be said that it stops short at the Sunday-
school stage. God, to a very great number of men, is an abstrac-
tion, a vague "One above." What is really lacking is a grasp of

the Christian view of God as proclaimed in the Incarnation.... But this is merely the negative side of the case. What is equally true and far more striking is the fact that the war itself has fostered in the lives of the vast majority of men qualities that are, to say the least, potentially Christian. The paradox appears, that in the hard school of reality men are finding true lessons which it is the peculiar duty of the Church to foster, and which they were either unwilling or unable to learn from the Church before the war.' The Rev. P. C. T. Crick, Fellow and Dean of Clare College, Cambridge, on pp. 360–1 of *The Church in the Furnace*.

7, p. 10. *A Lecture on the Study of History*, 1895, p. 63.

8, p. 10. Full details of this singular, though by no means unique, episode may be found in *The Church Quarterly* for Jan. 1901, pp. 291 ff. and in the 2nd edition of my first series of *Medieval Studies*, p. 79.

9, p. 11. Four quotations from three very different writers may be given to support the position taken here.

(*a*) J. H. Newman, *Essay on Development*, 1845, Introd. p. 5: 'It is melancholy to say it, but the chief, perhaps the only English writer who has any claim to be considered an ecclesiastical historian, is the infidel Gibbon.'

(*b*) Letter of J. H. Newman to Father Coleridge, S.J., dated July 24th, 1864: 'Nothing would be better than an Historical Review for Roman Catholics—but who would bear it? Unless one doctored all one's facts, one would be thought a bad Catholic' (*The Month*, Jan. 1903, p. 3).

(*c*) F. D. Maurice, Preface to C. Kingsley's *Saint's Tragedy*, 1848: 'The time is, I hope, at hand when those who are most in earnest will feel that therefore they are most bound to be just— when they will confess the exceeding wickedness of the desire to distort or suppress a fact, or misrepresent a character—when they will ask as solemnly to be delivered from the temptation to this, as to any crime which is punished by law. The clergy ought specially to lead the way in this reformation. They have erred grievously in perverting history to their own purposes. What was a sin in others was in them a blasphemy, because they professed to acknowledge God as the Ruler of the world, and hereby they shewed that they valued their own conclusions above the facts which reveal His order. They owe, therefore, a great *amende* to their country, and they should consider seriously how they can make it most effectually.'

(*d*) Dr C. Gore, Bishop of Oxford, in a sermon preached before the University of Cambridge, May 12, 1918: 'Men and women of quite different religious traditions...want to know why the Church has so largely and so long forgotten a great part of its true message—why it was left to a reputed atheist like Shelley, and to men rather far off orthodoxy like the authors of *Ecce Homo* and *The Jesus of History*, to present to us those undoubtedly historical aspects of the teaching of Jesus which appeal most to what is best in the modern world.'

**10, p. 13.** Beatus Jacobus de Marchia in Baluze-Mansi, *Miscellanea*, vol. ii. pp. 600, 609; cf. Bernardini Senensis *Opera*, vol. i. 1636, p. 6, col. 433 a, b. For the way in which the medieval cult of the miraculous led to equally pitiless deductions in another direction, see below, Lecture II, note 13.

**11, p. 16.** Tertullian, *Apologeticus*, § 15; cf. *De Testimonio Animae*, § 1 and Hieronymus, *ad Laetam*, § 1.

**12, p. 21.** W. Blake, Preface to *Milton*.

**13, p. 28.** The medieval mind oscillated between blind belief in miracles and an uncomfortable conviction that the age of real miracles was receding more and more into a distant background: both sides may be seen in St Gregory. Most significant in this context is the memorial drawn up for the ecumenic Council of Lyons in 1274 by the then General of the Dominicans, Humbert de Romans. He justifies the crusades on the ground that Christians are, in these days, driven by necessity to use the sword against unbelievers: for 'even as an artificer, when he has lost one tool, uses another that still remains to him, so we Christian folk, not having miracles now-a-days, but still possessing warlike weapons, defend ourselves with these latter.' Humbert was one of the most remarkable churchmen of the later thirteenth century; and his words are significant of the pagan state of mind to which miracle-worship logically leads (Mansi, *Concilia*, vol. 24, p. 114 a).

**14, p. 31.** See T. Patrick, *The Apology of Origen*, 1892, pp. 210 ff. Mr Patrick sums up truly: 'thus the moral argument took precedence of the miraculous, which lost its former precedence in the Christian consciousness, and was superseded though not altogether supplanted.'

**15, p. 36.** St Thomas Aquinas, for instance, seems to show here a great deal less than his usual love of thoroughness.

**16, p. 37.** Professor E. G. Browne notes the same significant, though natural, inconsistency among the Bábís: 'In spite of the official denial of the necessity, importance or evidential value of miracles in the ordinary sense, numerous miracles are recorded in Bábí histories....and many more are related by adherents of the faith' (*Materials for the Study of the Bábí Religion*, 1918, p. xxiii).

**17, p. 37.** See p. 73 of the most accessible edition (Cassell's *National Library*, vol. 11).

**18**, p. 42. The Rev. G. Rawlinson, *Bampton Lectures* (1859), pp. 50–51, quoted by T. H. Huxley, *Science and Hebrew Tradition,* p. 210. In the Roman catholic church biblical apologetics are naturally still more grotesque, since pope Pius X decreed the doctrine of biblical infallibility in an extreme form. Abbé A. Houtin exposed the folly of this doctrine by publishing a book which quoted freely from the absurdities of these apologists; although he abstained to a great extent from comment, and generally contented himself with printing the exact words of these writers, his book was finally placed on the Index; see A. Fawkes, *Studies in Modernism,* 1913, pp. 50, 55.

**19**, p. 48. E. G. Browne, *The New History of the Báb,* 1893, introd. pp. xxi–xxx, and *Materials for the Study of the Bábí Religion,* xxiii–xxiv. As Professor Browne points out, it is apparently by the merest accident that the original chronicle has survived at all.

**20**, p. 52. The most accessible source for the text of this letter is H. Böhmer, *Analekten zur Geschichte des Franciscus v. Assisi,* Tübingen, 1904, p. 90. The crucial passage runs: 'Non diu ante mortem frater et pater noster apparuit crucifixus quinque plagas, quae vere sunt stigmata Christi, portans in corpore suo: nam manus eius et pedes quasi puncturas clavorum habuerunt ex utraque parte confixas, reservantes [reserantes?] cicatrices et clavorum nigredinem ostendentes. Latus vero eius lanceatum apparuit et saepe sanguinem evaporavit. Dum adhuc vivebat spiritus eius in corpore, non erat in eo aspectus sed despectus, vultus eius, et nullum membrum in eo remansit absque nimia passione.' I cannot help suspecting that the *reservantes* of this passage should be *reserantes,* and have therefore translated accordingly. If however we keep *reservantes,* and therefore translate 'retaining the scars,' it makes no difference to the present argument. The phraseology of the last sentence is modelled on Isaiah liii. 2, 3. Celano is even more outspoken in his Second Life (§ 129, tr. Ferrers Howell, p. 266): 'he subjected his body, assuredly innocent, to scourgings and hardships, multiplying wounds upon it without cause.' Add to this the well-known confession recorded by the Three Companions (ch. iv. § 14). 'He confessed that he had sinned much [in austerity] against Brother Body.'

**21**, p. 53. I. Celano, § 95; Böhmer, p. 93.

**22**, p. 55. I. Celano, § 95, tr. A. G. Ferrers Howell (Methuen, 1908, p. 93). The original is also in Böhmer, p. 93; it runs: 'Manus et pedes eius in ipso medio clavis confixi videbantur, clavorum capitibus in interiori parte manuum et superiori pedum apparentibus et eorum acuminibus existentibus de adverso. Erant enim signa illa rotunda interius in manibus, exterius autem oblonga, et

178    CHRIST, ST FRANCIS AND TO-DAY

caruncula quaedam apparebat quasi summitas clavorum retorta et repercussa, quae carnem reliquam excedebat. Sic et in pedibus impressa erant signa clavorum et a carne reliqua elevata. Dextrum quoque latus quasi lancea transfixum cicatrice obducta erat, quod saepe sanguinem emittebat ita, ut tunicam eius cum femoralibus multoties respargeret sanguine sacro.'

**23**, p. 55. Bonaventura, *Legenda Major*, Miracula, 1. 2. *Little Flowers. Of the Most Holy Stigmata*, last chapter.

**24**, p. 56. I ought to have referred in this lecture, as I had done on similar occasions previously, to the well-known case of Louise Lateau, which is summarized on pp. 492–3 of F. W. H. Myers' *Human Personality*, etc., vol. 1. 1903, and which may very well have been a genuine case of auto-suggestion of stigmata. But, without excluding the possibility either of auto-suggestion or of miracle proper in St Francis's case, it is the historian's duty to indicate simpler solutions, if such can be found. It is unlikely that there will ever be general agreement upon such a case as this; meanwhile, however, it is a gain to discuss every possible alternative.

**25**, p. 56. The most exhaustive treatment of the evidence is in a monograph by J. Merkt, *Die Wundmale d. H. F. v. Assisi* (Teubner, 1910).

**26**, p. 57. *Nouvelles Etudes d'Histoire Religieuse*, 1884, p. 326.

**27**, p. 62. This appears clearly enough even from the writings of so orthodox a Trinitarian as the late Professor Gwatkin, though it would be most illegitimate to claim his great authority for the wider deductions which I have ventured to make. The following quotations from his *Studies of Arianism* (2nd ed. 1900) will illustrate the statement in my text:

p. 8. 'We find two great tendencies, each rooted deep in human nature, each working inside and outside the church, and each traversing the whole field of Christian doctrine....The first tendency was distinctly rationalistic. Its crude form of Ebionism had denied the Lord's divinity outright. And, now that this was accepted, it was viewed as a mere influence or power, or in any case as not divine in the highest sense. Thus the reality of the Incarnation was sacrificed, and the result was a clear reaction to the demigods of polytheism.'

p. 26. 'The Lord's deity had been denied often enough before, and so had his humanity; but it was reserved for Arianism at once to affirm and to nullify them both. The [*Arian*] doctrine is heathen to the core; for the Arian Christ is nothing but a heathen demigod.'

p. 27. 'No false system ever struck more directly at the life of Christianity than Arianism....Yet the work of Ulphilas is an abiding witness that faith is able to assimilate the strangest errors; and the conversion of the northern nations [to Arianism] remains in evidence that Christianity can be a power of life even in its most degraded forms.'

p. 28. 'Sabellius...had reduced the Trinity to three successive manifestations of the one God in the Law, the Gospel, and the church.'

p. 33. 'Arianism enabled [some heathens] to use the language of Christians without giving up their heathen ways of thinking.... Nor was the attraction only for nominal Christians like these. Careless thinkers—sometimes thinkers who were not careless—might easily suppose that Arianism had the best of such passages as "the Lord created me[1]" or "The Father is greater than I[2]...."

' Nor was even this all. The Lord's divinity was a real difficulty to thoughtful men. They were still endeavouring to reconcile the philosophical idea of God with the fact of the incarnation. In point of fact the two things are incompatible, and one or the other would have to be abandoned.... The Easterns were more inclined to theories of subordination, to distinctions of the derivately from the absolutely divine, and to views of Christ as a sort of secondary God. Such theories do not really meet the difficulty. A secondary God is necessarily a second God. Thus heathenism still held the key of the position and constantly threatened to convict them of polytheism. They could not sit still, yet they could not advance without remodelling their central doctrine of the divine nature to agree with revelation. Nothing could be done till the Trinity was placed inside the divine *nature*. But this is just what they could not for a long time see.'

Compare the same writer's words in the *Cambridge Medieval History*, vol. I. chap. v: 'Arius had no idea of starting a heresy; his only aim was to give a commonsense answer to the pressing difficulty that, if Christ is God, he is a second God.... As it appeared later, few agreed with him; but there were many who saw no reason for turning him out of the church. If the conservatives (who were the mass of the Eastern bishops) had signed the creed with a good conscience, they had no idea of making it their working belief. They were not Arians—or they would not have torn up the Arianizing creed at Nicæa; but if they had been hearty Nicenes, no influence of the Court could have kept up an Arianizing reaction for half a century. Christendom as a whole was neither Arian nor Nicene but conservative. If the East was not Nicene neither was it Arian, but conservative, and if the West was not Arian, neither was it Nicene but conservative also.'

[1] Prov. viii. 22, LXX. mistranslation.
[2] John xiv. 28.

It would, of course, be possible to support the statement in my text (which was questioned by two of my most competent critics) by still clearer quotations from such a book as Harnack's *History of Dogma*. But it seemed better to appeal to so orthodox an authority as Dr Gwatkin for proof of the assertion that, however few professing Christians might have repudiated the words *God* and *divine*, large numbers understood these words in a sense very different from that professed by the modern catholic. And, if this be so, then I have established my contention that some of the most fundamental doctrines of modern orthodoxy are not catholic in the sense of having been held *always* and *everywhere* by *all* Christians; so that the word *catholic*, under analysis, simply means *majoritarian*. For it would be useless even if we could prove that certain forms of words had always been repeated, so long as those forms were held by different Christians in senses so different that, when it came to the final conflict, the victorious majority often denied the name of Christian to the conquered minority. God, who is the object of our religion, regards not words but the inmost thoughts of the heart. Indeed, so little do words secure real uniformity, that one of my critics in the discussion which followed these lectures, while pressing upon me the Nicene creed, was obviously taken aback when I pointed out that it made Jesus God Almighty. The idea, when put into words slightly different from those of the creed, was startling even to this thoughtful and orthodox anglican; so true is it that even orthodoxy often fails to realize fully its most essential commitments.

Is there not a close parallel to this in the history of Papal Infallibility? Those who pressed for a definition in 1870 were able to bring very plausible evidence for their contention that the doctrine had been the belief of the Roman church for centuries, at least; the fact being, that people had become more and more accustomed to hearing the words used, and even to using them themselves in a loose sense, without accepting the full commitments of such a doctrine. But even those who would always have asserted the doctrine, in one form or another, against a protestant adversary, were in many cases most reluctant to risk a definition which, by putting an end to all ambiguities, committed the church to all the tremendous consequences of an absolute assertion.

**28**, p. 64. University Sermon of Oct. 20, 1918, by the Rev. J. P. Whitney, B.D., late Professor of Ecclesiastical History, King's College, London.

**29**, p. 65. Bossuet, *Œuvres*, vol. XII. (1816), pp. 1 ff.

**30**, p. 68. Bishop Gore, on pp. 29–30 of his *Basis of Anglican Fellowship*, appeals to the New Testament for proof of his own conception of the church; but, in the absence of clear definition, it

is difficult to give much weight to an appeal of this kind. Compare
F. J. A. Hort, *The Christian Ecclesia* (1897), p. 168. Dr Hort says,
writing of the Epistle to the Ephesians, 'it is true that, as we have
seen, St Paul anxiously promoted friendly intercourse and sympathy between the scattered Ecclesiae; but the unity of the
universal Ecclesia as he contemplated it does not belong to this
region; it is a truth of theology and of religion, not a fact of what
we call Ecclesiastical politics.'

**31**, p. 68. Moreover, in its earliest days the church had not
even clearly formulated such an aim. When bishop Gore claims
that the church is catholic because there can be in it 'neither Jew
nor Greek,' he ignores the fact that this question of the admission
of the uncircumcised caused a very serious division for some time
in the church, and that, if St Paul had failed and died during this
quarrel, majoritarianism would have branded him as a heretic
(*The Religion of the Church*, p. 40).

**32**, p. 70. Bishop Gore exaggerates this tendency quite un-
justifiably. When he claims for his own doctrine of the ministry 'an
extraordinary unanimity of judgment' [in the church], or 'astonish-
ing unanimity for more than 1500 years in Christendom,' and when,
again, he speaks of it as existing 'from the first,' he is really reading
backwards into the first years of Christianity the Ignatian conception of two generations later (*Religion of the Church*, pp. 70, 72;
*Basis*, pp. 29, 30). What fatal errors may lurk under this anachronism, I attempt to show in my fifth lecture. It may be added
that Dr. Gore uses the word *historical* in a very loose and inaccurate
sense: *e.g.*, on pp. 22, 26 of his *Basis*. The strictly *historical*
evidence there referred to is not such as would move a business
man or a jury to any important decision; both cases come far more
into the realm of moral than of historical evidence, as Origen saw
1600 years ago. Dr Gore thus comes to some extent under his own
frank condemnation: 'To proclaim an event in history without any
tolerable historical evidence, is to play into the hands of rationalism' (*ibid.* p. 45).

**33**, p. 71. This is curiously exemplified in a correspondence
which I came across only after these words were written. A
long and able review of the book came out in *The Times Literary
Supplement* for May 30, 1918, devoting two columns to a very
complimentary appreciation of Mr Turner's essay, and to certain
practical deductions which seemed to follow therefrom. A fort-
night later, Mr Turner printed a letter protesting that the reviewer
had almost altogether mistaken him, yet attempting only briefly,
and on only one point, to correct these mistakes in detail. The
reviewer replied that he would willingly stand corrected if more
could be proved against him; and to this Mr Turner rejoined

(June 27): 'I only wished to say, and I repeat, that the conclusions which the writer deduced from my essay were not in fact my own. ...I hope my reviewer will not think me churlish if I leave the matter here; I did my best to avoid controversy when writing the essay, and I am not going to be drawn into it now.' The rest of his letter did, in fact, studiously avoid distinct explanations as to the main point at issue between him and his reviewer—and, it may be added, the point which most practically interested the public.

It is impossible, of course, to suspect a scholar of Mr Turner's known courtesy of churlishness; but it may fairly be said that his reserve is not generous to the public at large. It is not comfortable to belong to a church in which Mr Williams is a type of the scholars who clearly commit themselves, while students of Mr Turner's caution and exhaustive learning decline either to enunciate any practical conclusion, or to tell us in any practical way where the reviewer is wrong. We have been waiting since Augustine for somebody who would lay down a doctrine of the church which should be at once clear enough for the practical man to live by, and accurate enough to stand the most elementary historical tests.

**34, p. 72.** 'The orthodox Greek church came to reckon the sacraments as seven owing to the influence of the West, i.e., gradually from the year 1274 onwards. Still the number seven never came to have the importance attached to it in the West' (A. Harnack, *Hist. of Dogma*, tr. Speirs, vol. IV. 1898, p. 278). To Dionysius the Areopagite there were six sacraments, and he makes monastic ordination a separate sacrament from priestly ordination (*ibid.* p. 277). Even St Augustine 'did not evolve a harmonious theory either of the number or notion of the sacraments,' *ibid.* vol. VI. p. 156.

**35, p. 75.** This statement caused such surprise among my audience that I give full references. Aquinas, *Summa Theologica*, Pars III. Quaest. LXVII. art. 5: 'One who has not himself been baptized may confer baptism in due ecclesiastical form and in case of necessity. If he were to baptize without such necessity, he would sin grievously, but would confer the sacrament of baptism'; cf. *ibid.* 2ª 2ᵃᵉ, Quaest. XXXII. art. 4: *resp. ad primum*; also index: 'any human being of either sex or any religion, even though he be a Jew or a Pagan, may baptize in case of necessity, if there be no fitter minister at hand.' St Thomas points out that Augustine left the question open, but that Canon Law had since decided it. Compare the later decree of Eugenius [IV], quoted in Migne's *Encyclopédie Théologique*, vol. IX. col. 272: 'In case of necessity, not only can priest or deacon baptize, but even layfolk and women; nay, even pagans or heretics, provided they keep the form of the church and intend to do what the church doth.' It is again explicitly asserted in the decrees of the council of Trent (Pars II. cap. ii. § 22 : Streitwolf and Klener, *Libri Symbolici*, vol. I. p. 270). The latest revision of Canon Law (1917), in spite of its extreme caution, is obliged to confess the same fact: 'Baptism...may be administered by anybody, so long as the due matter, form and intention be kept' (Canon 742, § 1).

**36**, p. 76. W. Martens, *Gregor. VII*. 1894, vol. I. p. 264; H. C. Lea, *History of Sacerdotal Celibacy*, 1907, vol. II. pp. 228-9 and notes. The fact that Gregory at another time seemed to decide differently as to simoniacal orders (Martens, vol. I. p. 306) only emphasizes the unapostolic vagueness which it is my main object in the text to point out. The same may be said of the modern plea that, when Gregory spoke of simoniacal ordinations as *invalid* (*irritae*), he only meant *irregular*; that he always recognized their sacramental validity and only insisted on their guilt. Such a defence assumes, on the part of this great pope, ignorance of the most elementary logical distinctions. These, on any working theory of apostolical succession, should have been cleared up beyond all possibility of doubt centuries before Gregory was born.

**37**, p. 77. 'We [chaplains] used to be rather apologetic about our religion [at the front], introducing it with subtle phrases of suggestion, like a politician wooing the votes of an unsympathetic electorate. In other cases our apology took the shape of truculence, as who should say "This is what I believe: take it or leave it as you like"—which really meant: "This is what I am going to believe, whether it's true or not." In each case we probably assumed the callousness or hostility of our audience: we certainly implied a disbelief in our own Gospel. All that is over now. We know that the Spirit of God in men's hearts makes them eager for a priesthood exercising its functions without a veil on its face...we know, in short, that we are wanted.' The Rev. K. E. Kirk, Tutor of Keble College, Oxford, on p. 419 of *The Church in the Furnace*. Compare the same writer's words on pp. 410–411: 'Hidden under the inarticulate religion of the British soldier of which so much has been written, lies a deep and intense reverence for the priesthood. ...So great is the demand for the priest and his ministry...that he has only to show himself in the slightest degree accessible, to be overwhelmed with appeals, overt or implied, for help. Here is a fragment from a wounded soldier's letter to the chaplain of his battalion: "Dear Sir, I often used to wish you would talk seriously and privately to me about religion, though I never dared to ask you, and I must admit I seemed to be very antagonistic when you did start."'

**38**, p. 78.  Immediately after writing these words, I came across a report of Canon Newbolt's Reunion sermon at St Paul's Cathedral (*Church Times*, Aug. 23, p. 131). A few quotations will illustrate my point better than anything else could do: 'The real issue which lies at the bottom of all schemes for the Reunion of Christians,' says Canon Newbolt, is this: 'The question which divides Christians at the present day is a question of truth, not a question of opinions. ...We are concerned with a truth, with a deposit which is given to us in trust, and which we are bound to hold. We believe that in the forty days which followed on His Resurrection, Christ Jesus formulated the system and order of what we know as the Church, while He spoke to His disciples of the things concerning the Kingdom of God, such as Holy Baptism, ordering them to observe all things whatsoever He had commanded them....And out of that teaching emerges the great conception of the Church which justifies its existence as a body divinely endowed with Heavenly gifts for the continual welfare of mankind in his struggle with the devil, the world, and the flesh, all through the ages until Christ comes again. These are things which the Church feels to be necessary, and things which cannot be given up.' The first thing to notice here is the usual combination of vagueness and dogmatism. On the one hand, the principle claims to be so absolute as to forbid all question of compromise, on the other hand, it is so loosely phrased that we may make it mean almost anything,' so long as we leave untouched the one central idea in the preacher's mind: '*I* am in the church: *j'y suis, j'y reste.*' The second point to notice is this: the idea that Jesus 'formulated the system and order' during the forty days is repudiated not only by the majority of historical scholars outside the catholic fold, but by some of the best scholars within it. To Loisy, it is almost as incredible as to Harnack: 'the first Christian group,' he says, 'was not yet conscious of forming a society distinct from Judaism' (*Ev. et Eglise*, 1904, p. 136). There may be no reason why canons and lay-folk should not caress the idea as a matter of private judgment based on post-biblical tradition; but there are many reasons why we should not permit such mere personal opinions to form an impassable barrier between us and our fellow-Christians.

**39**, p. 81.  Matth. x. 7 ff.; I. Celano, § 22.

**40**, p. 87.  *Archiv für Litteratur- und Kirchengeschichte des Mittelalters*, vol. i. p. 530; cf. ii. p. 319.

**41**, p. 87.  Baluze-Mansi, *Miscellanea*, vol. ii. pp. 248 and 271.

**42**, p. 88.  He himself only knew Latin 'after a fashion' (I. Cel. I. § 22). He would not allow a novice to possess a psalter (*Mirror*, c. 4); and chap. 10 of the Rule of 1223 prescribes 'let not those brethren who know not letters try to learn them.'

# NOTES

185

**43,** p. 89. *Compendium Studii Philosophiae*, R. S. 1859, p. 426. The late Father R. H. Benson blundered badly in attempting to *contrast* the friars with 'the studious orders' (*Cambridge History of English Literature*, vol. III. p. 49). There was far more intellectual life among the thirteenth century friars than in any other order.

**44,** p. 90. Leading Article of May 3, 1918.

**45,** p. 90. *The Basis of Anglican Fellowship*, 1914, p. 30.

**46,** p. 91. 'But, for the most part, the liberal Catholic...does not value the sacraments and outward privileges of a Catholic less, because he recognizes that internal is more necessary than external union with the church, and that "the unleavened bread of sincerity and truth" is more essential to the soul than even the sacramental bread of life.' G. Tyrrell, *Through Scylla and Charybdis*, 1907, p. 81.

**47,** p. 94. *Œuvres de Leibniz*, ed. A. Foucher de Careil, t. II. (1860), p. 385; cf. Introd. p. lxviii.

**48,** p. 94. *Ibid.* Introd. pp. lxxix ff., 429 ff. Foucher de Careil, who as a Roman catholic takes Bossuet's side up to this point, confesses frankly here that Bossuet must have received 'this last and triumphant reply of Leibnitz'; that he did not answer it; and that his nephew very likely suppressed it, when preparing Bossuet's papers for publication, in order to make it appear that his uncle had had the last word. This was, in fact, the general belief until Foucher de Careil completed the correspondence from Leibnitz's own papers.

**49,** p. 94. *Ibid.* p. 439. It might be well to quote the words immediately preceding, which Lord Acton has pencil-marked for emphasis in his own copy (Cambs. Univ. Library, Acton, c. 51. 354). 'Où sont ces fondemens prétendus solides dont messieurs de Trente se sont servis pour innover sur le canon avec tant de hardiesse? Est-ce la tradition? Point du tout. Le contraire a esté receu autresfois. Sont-ce quelques nouvelles descouvertes, quelque vieux manuscrit, quelque ancien monument? On n'en connoist point. C'est donc quelque nouvelle inspiration du Sainct-Esprit. Mais ces messieurs ont-ils esté des gens à inspiration? On ne doit point cesser de souffrir la doctrine que l'ancienne Église a jugée supportable, et encore moins celle qu'elle a constamment enseignée.'

**50,** p. 94. *Ibid.* p. 349; cf. 289. Leibnitz concludes with the very pertinent reflection 'tant il est important d'éviter le relaschement, mesme dans les manieres de parler.'

**51,** p. 95. A friendly criticism has enabled me here to modify the too unqualified statement of my original lecture.

The real difficulty, from first to last, lies in the confusion of terms. From early Christianity down to the Council of Trent, at least, it was acknowledged that there existed two classes even among the books which were peculiarly sacred. Some were of *dogmatic* authority, while others, though also authoritative, were only of *persuasive* force; the latter deserved high respect, and might even be publicly read in church, but the former were of such authority that all Christians were bound to believe whatever they explicitly asserted, and to obey whatever they explicitly prescribed. This distinction is very clearly marked nowadays by two technical terms; the books of supreme authority are called *protocanonical* and the others *deuterocanonical*. But no such clear terminology was adopted during the first fifteen Christian centuries, so that it is often quite impossible to decide whether a father, a council, or a pope is speaking of the first or of the second class; and this fact, in itself, would almost seem sufficient to rob the doctrine of apostolical succession of all *practical* value. I underline this word, because some of my hearers evidently did not notice the important distinction it implies. No doubt there are certain *academic* senses in which the theory of apostolical succession can be defended; but those senses differ little, under ultimate analysis, from such theories of ecclesiastical evolution as even an agnostic might admit or propound. The only sense in which I am concerned with apostolic·succession is that indicated in my fourth lecture—the intensely practical question: Does there exist any authority, here on earth, sufficiently clear in its constitution and in its decrees to assure us of a true answer when we consult it on any religious question of primary importance? Is there any body, singular or plural, whom I can safely follow if he or they insist, for instance, that I must accept implicitly any particular miracle recorded in the gospels, or that I must abstain from ecclesiastical communion with certain fellow-Christians?

If any clear authority of this kind has come down from the apostles, it seems impossible to account for the actual history of the Bible canon, not only till the council of Trent but till the present day. Christ himself insisted on the binding force of the Old Testament scriptures; which, then, were these scriptures by which all Christians were to be bound? Athanasius, Jerome, Gregory the Great (to name only three out of many) give lists which even catholic apologists admit to be irreconcilable with the Tridentine canon. Jerome's judgment is of peculiar significance, not only because he was indisputably the best biblical scholar among the western fathers, but also because his words still stand in the preface to the Vulgate. He put them there, he tells us, as 'a sort of military sentry,' to warn his readers that 'whatsoever is outside these books, must be counted among the apocrypha:

therefore *Wisdom* (commonly called Solomon's) and the book of *Jesus Son of Sirach*, and *Judith*, and *Tobit*, and the *Pastor* [of Hermas], are not in the canon.' He could scarcely have been more explicit; yet even this clear testimony is immensely reinforced by that of his great adversary Rufinus, who would have been only too glad to catch Jerome tripping. So far is Rufinus from dissenting on this point, that he is one of our most explicit witnesses on the same side. We have received, he says, 'according to the tradition of our forefathers,' certain books which 'are believed to be inspired by the Holy Ghost himself'; and he then gives a list agreeing with Jerome and with the protestant Bible, except that Baruch goes with Jeremiah. He then continues: 'Yet thou must know that there are other books also which our forefathers called not *canonical* but *ecclesiastical*; *i.e. Wisdom* called Solomon's [and, in short, the books counted by protestants among the Apocrypha]. All which books they did indeed wish to be read in their churches, but not to be brought forward for the confirmation of the authority of faith [by quotations] from them.' He ends by asserting again that he has the authority of church tradition for this list. Augustine, it is true, and two African councils under his influence, gave a list of canonical books including those which Jerome and many others so expressly excluded. But (1) even if the authorities were equal on both sides, this would only show either (*a*) that Christ had never thought of telling the apostles distinctly which were, and which were not, to be reckoned among the strictly inspired books of the Old Testament—which were in fact those books of the Law and Prophets which Christ had come to fulfil—or (*b*) that the apostles, having once known this, either forgot it themselves or allowed it to fall into oblivion. In any case, the church remained in doubt, for fifteen centuries at least, as to a question which may almost be said to lie at the very root of Christian theology, and which (if St Jerome is right) could at any time have been set at rest, for all eternity, in three sentences filling eight lines of ordinary print.

(2) But the authorities are *not* equally balanced. The greatest medieval scholars are found far more frequently, more or less explicitly, on Jerome's side, from John of Salisbury and Thomas Aquinas down to Cardinal Cajetan who died in 1534. A full list may be found in F. Kaulen's *Einleitung in die Heilige Schrift* (2nd ed., 1884), vol. i. p. 23; Kaulen was a Roman catholic professor who published with the express approbation of the archbishop of Freiburg.

(3) And, more important still, whereas the 'excluders,' as we may call Jerome's party, draw quite clear distinctions, and often give their reasons (Rufinus, for instance, who appeals emphatically to ecclesiastical tradition), the other side are far more vague. The only solemn papal pronouncement which Kaulen is able to quote

(Damasus, A.D. 374) merely undertakes to give a list of the 'divine scriptures, [to show] which the universal catholic church receives, and which she should avoid.' But it is notorious that 'divine scriptures' was a loose term covering even books admitted to be only deuterocanonical; *e.g.* it is applied to *The Shepherd* by another pope (T. Zahn, *Geschichte des Neutestamentlichen Kanons*, 1888, vol. I, p. 346). Moreover, both Kaulen (p. 25) and the *Catholic Encyclopedia* (vol. IV. p. 272) admit that this papal list 'did not possess any general binding force,' and that there was no authoritative ecclesiastical definition until 1565 A.D. Of all the popes who came between Jerome and the council of Trent, not one dared publicly to stigmatize Jerome's explicit assertion as incorrect, or even to expunge it silently as incorrect from the preface to the Vulgate. And St Augustine's catalogue, which at first sight seems to contradict Jerome's so clearly, is really far from this temerity (*De Doctrina Christiana*, lib. II. c. 8). He comes to the subject of 'canonical scriptures'—a term which was sometimes loosely used to cover both protocanonical and deuterocanonical—and he tells us expressly that these 'canonical scriptures' are of different degrees of authority; that some are received by all churches, and others rejected by some of the churches. The Christian, he says, must estimate these books more or less highly according to the number and weight of the churches which receive or reject them. He then proceeds to recite 'the whole canon of scriptures to which this consideration is to be applied'; and then gives a list including Jerome's proto- and deuterocanonical books without further distinction. But the very distinction from which he started warns us, almost as clearly as Jerome had warned us, against lumping all these books together in a single category. It seems plain enough that Augustine could not trust himself—not being a specialist in biblical scholarship, and having a natural conservative desire to accept as much as possible of what he found in the Vulgate—to decide clearly in each case between proto- and deuterocanonical books; but it seems equally clear that he knew his list included both categories; why else should he warn us to distinguish between the authority of one book or another, and to judge for ourselves according to the suffrages for or against individual books?

It seemed worth while to enter so far into a rather technical subject, because the history of the Bible canon bears almost as directly upon the question of apostolical succession as on the failure of Leibnitz's religious concordat.

**52**, p. 99. The tragedy of Christian exclusiveness is somewhat relieved by the comedy of Anglo-catholic and Roman catholic rivalry in this matter. While the best minds are naturally alien to all that is narrow in this doctrine, and accept it only under pressure of relentless logic, a good many vulgar natures find real attraction in it, and welcome it even as a social force; if one must accept any church, it is *comme il faut* to belong to an older and more exclusive body than one's fellow-Christian. The following three quotations throw light on different sides of this problem.

(*a*) *The Month*, the Roman catholic monthly organ (Jan. 1903, p. 15; letter of J. H. Newman to Fr. Coleridge, Nov. 24, 1865).

'I cannot help feeling sorrow at the blow struck by the Holy Office at the members of the A.P.U.C.*'

(*b*) *The Church in the Furnace*, p. 117 (Canon M. Linton Smith, D.S.O.). After speaking of the good relations between Anglican and nonconformist chaplains, the writer proceeds: 'It were much to be wished that as much could be said for relations with the Roman communion. The contemptuous refusal of permission to use if only the naves of the churches for services will not be soon forgotten.... It has doubled, and more than doubled, the work of Church of England chaplains, who have often had to duplicate their services because there was no building, apart from the church, large enough to accommodate their congregation.' He goes on to give two even worse instances of the callousness of Roman catholic priests to Anglican burials.

(*c*) From a letter of the Dean of Worcester to *The Times* of Aug. 22, 1918. 'I would venture to ask those who think [that we must defer cooperation till all Churches accept Episcopacy] to ponder what is being done in the way of cooperation among the Churches in the United States in connexion with the war. According to a recent number of the *Federal Bulletin*, the War Department has established a large Training School for Chaplains. The faculty includes an Episcopalian, a Methodist Episcopal, a Baptist, a Roman Catholic. In the last entry into the school 30 were Methodists, 26 Roman Catholics, 15 Baptists, 15 Presbyterians, five Lutherans, two Congregationalists. "With the greatest good fellowship they work and study and confer together."' The cooperation in the Navy is still more striking. Secretary Daniels has recently appointed the Rev. M. C. Gleeson Chaplain of the Fleet. He is a Roman Catholic, and has been recommended for the post by both Protestant and Roman Catholic chaplains. More remarkable still, 'His duties will be to inspect all chaplains of the Fleet, of

* *Editor's note.*

The A P. U. C., or Association for the Promotion of the Unity of Christendom, in which Catholics and Anglicans joined to promote the cause of Corporate Reunion between their Churches, was condemned by the Roman Inquisition (November 8, 1865) as tending to countenance the claim of the Church of England to be a true branch of Christ's Church, and thus on a par with the communion of Rome.

all denominations, and their work, to advise them of matters that may be for the good of the Service, and to call meetings of all the chaplains in the fleet when necessity arises.' We are not yet ready for such cooperation in Great Britain, but it is well for us to realize that it can exist without compromising a man's loyalty to his own branch of the church. The war is making men increasingly impatient of emphasis on sectarian differences, and more than ever desirous that all who 'profess and call themselves Christians' should recognize as the one great essential that spiritual bond of union which results from belief in Jesus Christ.

**53,** p. 100. 'For my own part, I may say in passing, if I am to judge by the fruits of religion as I see them in life, I should be disposed to rank the Friends among the highest in the Kingdom of God; and they have no ministry and no sacraments' (The Bishop of Oxford [C. Gore], *The Basis of Anglican Fellowship,* 1914, p. 40).

**54,** p. 104. The Franciscan, Berthold of Regensburg, who flourished about 1250 A.D. and was one of the greatest of all medieval mission-preachers, is among our most emphatic witnesses on this point, to which he frequently recurs. The following quotation is from F. Pfeiffer's edition, 1862, vol. I. p. 393: 'Fie, penny-preacher, murderer of all the world, how many souls dost thou hurl, through thy false gains, from God's sunlight down to the bottomless pit, where they are past all hope! Thou promisest so much pardon for a single penny or halfpenny, that many thousands trust therein and dream that they have atoned for all their sins with this penny or halfpenny, as thou pratest to them. So they will never repent, but go hence to hell and are lost for ever.... Thou murderer of true penitence, thou hast murdered true penitence, which is one of the highest of God's seven sacraments.'

**55,** p. 104. *Select Discourses of John Smith,* 1859, p. 26.

**56,** p. 105. *Moralium in Job,* lib. XXVIII. c. vii. § 16. An even more liberal view of virtual Christianity is expressed by Justin Martyr in his *First Apology,* § XLVI.: 'We have already proved him [Christ] to be the firstborn of God and the Logos, of which mankind have all been partakers; and those who lived by reason were Christians, notwithstanding they were thought to be atheists. Such among the Greeks were Socrates and Heraclitus, and those like them.'

**57,** p. 105. Since writing the above, I have come upon the same conviction that everything worth having is a risk, far more vividly expressed, in *The Church in the Furnace,* pp. 429 ff. (Essay by the Rev. E. S. Woods, Examining Chaplain to the Bishop of Durham). Mr Woods insists that God even took risks in becoming man.

'What else was it but a huge adventure when Love came forth from the tents of Eternity to woo and win the heart of humanity? In a world of free men the result of the Incarnation could never have been a foregone conclusion.' Cf. p. 445: 'Perhaps the most important of these [tasks] for us to do is *to recover this sense that Christianity is an Adventure*, an enterprise, a Crusade.' Compare *ibid.* p. 186 (the Rev. E. Milner-White, Fellow of King's College, Cambridge): 'And this leads on to a third element. that the Church show some of the courage and decision of the Trenches, and be bold to *experiment.*' The italics in both cases are the authors' own.

**58**, p. 105. *Apologia pro Vita Sua*, ed. 1880, pp. 102, 104, 191, 198, 203-4, 243-4, 261. The clearest statement, perhaps, is that on p. 198: 'I came to the conclusion that there was no medium in true philosophy, between Atheism and Catholicity.' Cf. his letter to Henry Wilberforce in Wilfrid Ward's *Life of Cardinal Newman*, 1912, vol. I. p. 81: 'When a person feels that he cannot stand where he is, and has dreadful feelings lest he should be suffered to go back, if he will not go forward, such a case as Blanco White's increases those fears. For years I have had an increasing intellectual conviction that there is no medium between Pantheism and the Church of Rome.' This was written in 1845, when Newman was composing his *Essay on Development*.

**59**, p. 106. *Phaedo*, 90, Jowett's *Plato*, II. p. 235; 85, p. 229.

**60**, p. 107. Sermon VII. *Upon the Character of Balaam.*

**61**, p. 108. G. F. Bradby, *Some Verses*, 'Il Gran Rifiuto.'

**62**, p. 111. 'L'idée qu'en abandonnant l'Eglise, je resterais fidèle à Jésus, s'empara de moi; et, si j'avais été capable de croire aux apparitions, j'aurais certainement vu Jésus me disant: *Abandonne-moi pour être mon disciple.*' E. Renan, *Souvenirs d'Enfance et de Jeunesse*, 1883, p. 312.

**63**, p. 112. 'I am quite prepared to see such large developments in the coming form of Christianity that the religion of our sons and grandsons would seem to be almost another faith if it were witnessed by our grandfathers. But in fact they too will inherit the same faith, understood to be living and dynamic, and set forth to men in such a way as to meet the needs of our time.' *The Church in the Furnace*, p. 51, article by Rev. F. R. Barry, D.S.O., Fellow and Lecturer in Theology, Oriel Coll. Oxon.

**64**, p. 116. Compare the bishop of Oxford's testimonial to the Society of Friends quoted above (note 53).

**65**, p. 118. In 1901, in answer to some extraordinarily misleading statistics published by Mgr J. S. Vaughan, brother of the late Cardinal, I worked out the latest figures available (*Statesman's*

*Yearbook* for 1900). These are borne out by those of the *Yearbook* for 1917, where the figures between 1910 and 1914 work out roughly at 359,200 illegitimates yearly to 4,221,000 births in Roman catholic states, and 245,950 to 3,288,000 in protestant. The proportions per 1,000 are thus 85·1 and 74·8; *i.e.* 100 Roman catholic illegitimates to 87·2 protestant. Those who are curious to learn how Roman catholic writers of repute try to get at different results, may refer to the *Spectator* for Aug. 30, 1902, p. 291.

**66**, p. 119. By a strange coincidence, p. 291 of the same journal supplies evidence for this point also. Mr W. D. Gainsford, of Skendleby Hall, Spilsby, wrote to protest against religious tolerance. He argued 'the common-sense of the matter is that we are justified in constraining others for their own good (1) when we are reasonably certain that we are right, and (2) when we are physically able to do it. The real reason why religious persecution is unpopular to-day is that nobody is strong enough to persecute.' He was naturally disavowed by one or two other Roman catholic correspondents; but I believe I am right in saying (*a*) that none of these held any official position, and (*b*) that none of them pleaded any change in Roman church *law* on this subject since the middle ages.

Aquinas's doctrine on the subject is a moderate statement of the official medieval position (*Summa Theologica*, 2ᵃ 2ᵃᵉ, Quaest. x. and xi.). He divides the 'infideles' into three categories only—Pagans, Jews, and Heretics. A Pagan or a Jew must not be coerced to believe, but a heretic may. Heretics are 'those who profess the Christian faith, but corrupt its dogmas.' So long as the heretic has never had the catholic faith explained to him, he is of course excusable. But one who, having heard the priest's exposition of catholicism, refuses to accept it, is a heretic in the truest sense; he must recant or be handed over to the secular arm for capital punishment. Aquinas was, of course, familiar with cases where whole populations had been born and nurtured in heresy, as in modern times; but neither he nor his fellow-theorists make allowance for this, nor was it allowed for in inquisitorial practice. The Jesuit Father Rickaby, on p. 7 of his *Oxford Conferences* for 1897, attempts to argue otherwise, but cites no authority beyond a note which *he himself* had appended to his own abbreviated translation of Aquinas's book, in defiance of all medieval evidence! I pointed this out on p. 401 of *The Spectator* for Sept. 20, 1902; this led to a correspondence in *The Tablet* in which no attempt was made to justify Father Rickaby on this point.

Even before Aquinas, Innocent III in a great ecumenical council had decreed in the same sense (4th Lateran Council, A.D. 1215, cap. 3). Heretics everywhere are to be sought out with all diligence, and handed over to the secular arm. Princes who refuse to 'exterminate*' all heretics on their territory are to be deposed, and their lands given to others more faithful. There is no word of indulgence for heretics who had sucked in their present faith with their mothers' milk, though this decree was mainly aimed at the Albigenses, of whom a large proportion, and probably the majority, must have been in this case.

This decree, again, is indissolubly linked up with modern canon law, though of course nobody attempts to enforce it. The Creed of Pope Pius IV is still binding on all the Roman clergy, and is used as the official test even for layfolk: converts have to profess complete belief in this creed at their reception into the Roman church. The seventeenth article runs: 'I receive unhesitatingly [*indubitanter*] all things handed down, defined, and decreed by the sacred canons and the ecumenical councils, and especially by the holy council of Trent.' In strict canon law, therefore, Mr Gainsford was quite right as against his fellow-catholics, and might have silenced them at any moment if he had known what had been printed at Rome only a few months before he wrote. Father Marianus de Luca, S.J., was (and perhaps still is) professor of Canon Law at the papal university of Rome. A work in two volumes was published by him in 1901 at the Roman *Libraria Pontificia*, which has branches in Germany and America. The title is '*Institutiones Juris Ecclesiastici publici*...as delivered in public lectures at the papal university.' The covers of the book not only contain very flattering quotations from orthodox journals—'clearness of style' and 'profundity of doctrine,' 'drawn from the most famous Fathers and Doctors of the Church,' 'which have already excited the admiration of all who have followed his course of lectures,' etc. —but also a long and warm testimonial-letter from Pope Leo XIII to the author. On p. 258 of vol. 1. de Luca comes to deal with 'The Church's Power over Heretics.' He defines heretics as 'those who have been duly baptized, but who pertinaciously adhere to some error concerning the faith.' Of such people he concludes, as medieval writers had concluded, that they are subject to the laws of the [Roman] church, 'since they still bear the foundation of their subjection, which is the character of baptism.' Contrary arguments are lightly brushed aside: 'if heretics were not subjected to ecclesiastical jurisdiction, they could not even be punished by the church for their heresy: but [we know that] they *can* be so punished....Bellarmine rightly said that heretics were not *in* the church, but *belonged to* the church, since (1) they are subject to her jurisdiction, and (2) they are obliged to return to her.' On the next page he cites with approval Bellarmine's proofs of these assertions

---

* In Aquinas, *loc. cit.* Quaest. XI. art. 3, *conclusio*, 'exterminate' is used as equivalent to 'remove from the world by death.'

'(a) from the Bible (especially St Matthew, chap. 18); (b) from the decrees and laws of the [Roman] emperors, which the church has always approved.... Valentinian and Marcian decreed that all should be slain who attempt to teach evil [prava]; (c) from the laws of the church herself.. .,and (d) from the testimony of the Fathers.' Thése citations, it need hardly be said, are correct, and suffice of themselvçs to prove that the law of the church has remained essentially the same on this point for many centuries.

On p. 261 de Luca reminds his hearers of the orthodox arguments which justify the death penalty: '(1) because they [heretics] may lawfully be excommunicated, which is a greater punishment; (2) because this is sometimes the only remedy; (3) because forgers and (4) adulterers deserve death; but heretics are forgers of God's word, and adulterers who break faith with God, which is worse than breaking faith with a wife; (5) lest the evil do harm to the good, and the innocent be oppressed by the guilty; (6) in order that, by the execution of a few, the many may be corrected; (7) because it is sometimes better for the delinquents themselves; for these, being utterly obstinate, would only become worse the longer they lived, and would suffer still more excruciating pains in the flames of hell.'

To the plea that modern heretics are not in the church, and that all this legislation is irrelevant to such people, he replies with a downrightness which would have been very painful to his brother-Jesuit, Father Rickaby, if the latter had studied the subject deeply enough to come across these official lectures. 'I answer that, though heretics be not in the church, yet they ought to be, and therefore they pertain thereunto, as they pertain to the fold whence they have fled.... The church has in fact decreed many penalties against heretics... including that of death, which no man may escape who has been given over by the church to the secular arm. To this penalty not only are those subject who, after the age of reason, have fallen away from the faith, but those also who, once baptized, and growing up in heresy, defend pertinaciously that which they sucked in with their mothers' milk.'—*Huic poenae subjiciuntur non modo qui iam adulti a fide defecerunt, sed et qui baptizati, crescentes haeresim cum lacte matris haustam pertinaciter tuentur.* In the next pages, de Luca points out that this *legal right* of the church is unaffected by the fact that she often finds it *inopportune* to assert her jurisdiction over heretics. But the instances he gives are only from the matrimonial laws; he does not venture to allege anything which would imply a real change of policy on the subject of tolerance. Indeed Pius IX, in 1873, had expressly claimed to override laws made by the German emperor for his own subjects, on the ground that 'all who have received baptism belong (in a certain relation and manner which I need not

here specify) to the pope.' The fact that this was written in
defence of German catholics does not affect the principle on which
the pope bases his claim; and the emperor William replied bluntly
repudiating 'this assertion that all baptized folk belong to the
pope.' (L. Hahn, *Geschichte des Kulturkampfes*, 1881, p. 131.)

Moreover, such intolerance is justified not only by canon law,
but by inexorable logic, when once the ultramontane premisses are
granted. De Luca's mentality is clearly explained by that of his
older contemporary Giovanni Perrone, who was one of the great
doctors of the modern Roman church (1794–1876). He played a
leading part in the formal discussions which led to the decrees
of Immaculate Conception and Papal Infallibility; and his official
importance may be realized from the index to W. Ward's *Life of
Cardinal Newman*. His *Theological Lectures*, in nine volumes, ran
through thirty-four editions, and the abridged work ran through
forty-seven. He has been translated into at least eight languages.
One of the most widely-diffused of his writings was a little *Popular
Catechism dealing with Protestantism and the Catholic Church*, which
received official approbation in 1854. The whole book is a logical
outcome of Bossuet's position that those who are certain of their
apostolical succession have no moral right to make one single
concession to others who differ from them; and it leads equally
logically to Mr Gainsford's and canon de Luca's thesis. Here is
a specimen from chap. xv.

'*D*. Can those who pass from the catholic church to protestantism have this [excuse of] invincible ignorance?

*R*. The mere thought is absurd.... It is a contradiction and an
impossibility that any catholic should turn protestant through
honest motives; we might as well talk of committing a grievous
and heinous sin from honest motives.

*D*. Would you therefore say that no catholic who turns protestant can ever be saved?

*R*. I say that it is certain, with the certainty of faith, that all
catholics who turn to protestantism are damned, except those cases
where a man repents sincerely before his death and abjures the
errors he has professed. Except for such a case as this, it is an
article of faith that all catholics who become protestants are
damned irremediably for all eternity.

*D*. Why do you say that this damnation is one of the *certainties
of faith*?

*R*. Because it is a plain revelation of God.'

When we judge men's different conceptions of God after Christ's
test, 'by their fruits ye shall know them,' is it not absolutely necessary to take account of the fact that Perrone's and de Luca's words
were approved by the highest ecclesiastical authorities within the
memory of living man, and that the official church has never

dared publicly to revoke the barbarous legal enactments which followed logically from similar convictions?

**67**, p. 120. This point was constantly pressed by Leibnitz upon his Roman catholic correspondents who talked of reunion, yet refused to consider seriously whether the council of Trent might not be false in its claim to ecumenicity and infallibility. To Bossuet Leibnitz wrote in 1693, after urging the necessity of such a reconsideration: 'Si vous ne rejetez point cette thèse, monseigneur, que nous considérons comme la base de la négociation pacifique, il y aura moyen d'aller bien avant; mais, sans cela, nous nous consolerons d'avoir fait ce qui dépendoit de nous, et le blâme du schisme restera à ceux qui auront. refusé des conditions raisonnables.' To other correspondents he wrote still more plainly. (*Œuvres*, ed. A. Foucher de Careil, 1859, vol. I. p. 455; cf. pp. 163, 233, 330.)

For the false theology which underlies a false metaphor in the popular ecclesiastical use of this word *schism* see Prof. Kırsopp Lake, *The Heritage of Faith*, p. 172. Schism in Greek means *tearing*; it is applicable enough to a dead thing, like a garment; indeed, the metaphor is often expanded into a phrase: 'tearing the seamless robe of Christ.' Living organisms, on the other hand, multiply by division: each part goes on with a life of its own, and the sum of the organisms thus produced is far greater than any possibilities that lay before the individual parent. The student of church history, especially, has every reason to rejoice that we no longer live in the days of one undivided European hierarchy, even though that were the church of his own birth and nurture. There is divine unity; but there is a unity of the devil also. Can we find any word of bitterer indignation in the whole Bible than Jeremiah's condemnation of unity in error? 'A wonderful and horrible thing is committed in the land: the prophets prophesy falsely, and the priests bear rule by their means, and my people love to have it so.' (v. 30.)

**68**, p. 121. An able article from the high church point of view by Dr W. H. Frere, *The Christian Church in a Democracy*, may be found in *The Church Times* of March 8, 1918. Even those who may least agree with some of the writer's conclusions cannot fail to recognize the care he has taken to face both sides of this question.

**69**, p. 122. The stimulating journalist who contributes weekly to *The Church Times* over the signature *Viator* bears interesting testimony here from his own point of view (July 31, 1918, p. 397, col. 3). He quotes a doubting friend as writing to him 'I seem to have no use for any but the Christian religion, and that I cannot have'; and again, just before, 'I wish that — and — ' [the blanks stand for certain modernists] 'would openly confess that their religion is not the religion of the Christian Church.' The words would seem equally indicative of (1) the very prevalent desire for some form of Christianity and (2) the great danger of identifying 'the religion of the Christian Church' with the so-called catholic creed of to-day. Those who insist that the two must stand or fall together are appealing to the easiest, but the most dangerous of all arguments.

**70, p. 123.** Compare the words of an Anglican chaplain quoted in note 37.

**71, p. 130.** Most readers of Dr Gore's *Basis of Anglican Fellowship* will probably find his defence of these tests the weakest part of the little book (pp. 11, 17–19). The modernist, for instance, asks no more than to be allowed to treat the New Testament as Dr Gore confessedly treats the Old on p. 18.

**72, p. 130.** See the bishop of Hereford's letter to *The Times* of Aug. 17, 1918.

**73, p. 131.** H. Ellis, *A Study of British Genius*, 1904, pp. 77 ff.: 'The proportion of distinguished men and women contributed from among the families of the clergy can only be described as enormous' (*ibid.* p. 80).

**74, p. 132.** Since I have often quoted the bishop of Oxford to emphasize points of difference, justice demands an open confession of agreement with him as to the indefensibility of serious and continued mental reservation. The general public will have even less sympathy, if possible, with modernist clergy who go on repeating the old formulas, than with catholics who claim for those formulas an altogether unreal sanction.

**75, p. 134.** *Doctrine and Development*, 1898, pp. 128 ff.

**76, p. 135.** See note 69 above.

**77, p. 137.** More truly, of course, that which God discovers to us. To the Christian, God is seeking him even more than he is seeking God, and the non-Christian recognizes something like the same truth: that our environment is daily forcing upon us a thousand realities which even the most determined seekers constantly miss. Of all the half-wilful misconceptions in theology, few are more mischievous than the quiet assumption that those who repudiate tsarism in Christianity are therefore religious anarchists. When Christ refused to pronounce a ukase as to his own messianic character, and left John Baptist's disciples to find this out for themselves, he was not directing them to the more irresponsible but to the more responsible course of life. If they considered and decided that question in the real light of conscience, as ever in their great taskmaster's eye, then they did so with constant reference to God's will, and with anxious attention to every hint that seemed to come from God. I have already pointed out that, if we are to judge from insincere professors of either party, the Roman and Anglo-catholics will not get' the better of the comparison; common sense, as well as common fairness, demands that we should not assume an adversary's insincerity in default of real evidence. The following sentence from *The Church Times* of May 31, 1918 (p. 396, col. 2) is typical of the way in which this invidious assumption is exploited against non-catholics: 'To be independent, each one the framer of his and her creed, is to carry everywhere the portable idol of ourselves.' I have never met any Christian who proposed to frame his own creed in this sense: each is attempting to find the real Christ, and only so far 'after his own fashion' as he believes Christ would wish each man to form for himself an individual, and therefore a living, creed. The Jesuit Father Rickaby starts from exactly the same premisses as *The Church Times* to palliate the burning of heretics in former days (*Oxford Conferences*, 1897). Both writers are in fact confusing politics with religion. The state is constantly obliged to sweep aside conscientious objections, because the state is confessedly unable to read men's hearts, and can only judge by what it considers to be their social or anti-social conduct. But in this matter of faith we all admit that God is the real judge: and it would seem a curious impiety to argue as if God were incapable of judging except after our own rough and ready rules, or as if he were unwilling to guide the really sincere seeker.

But (the catholic will perhaps retort) no really sincere seeker will neglect the witness of the church in this matter. Exactly; but we do not necessarily neglect the witness of the church when we decline to rule our inner conscience after the decrees of those who, in our generation, claim to be the church. No true seeker will neglect to study, according to his powers, that which the church has done and thought in the past: but it is the modernist complaint that few people are so hopelessly ignorant of real church history as the so-called catholics. This is brought out with inimitable force by Loisy in his *Autour d'un Petit Livre*, pp. xi, 24 ff. Monsignor Duchesne, the catholic church historian of our own day who commands most general respect among historical scholars, has lived to see his greatest work put upon the Index, while the cardinal who deliberately reprinted gross misstatements (see p. 10) has himself claimed his elevation to the cardinalate as an official Papal tribute to his work in the historical field.

78, p. 139. Origen, *Contra Celsum*, lib. vii. (ed. G. Spencer, 1677, p. 362): 'For what man of sound sense would not laugh at that [pagan] who, after all these learned philosophical discussions concerning God or the gods, looks up to graven images and either offers prayers to them, or imagines that by contemplating them he must needs rise from the earthly and visible symbols to the truths of thought which these represent? Whereas the Christian, even the unlearned Christian, is convinced that every part of the world is a part of the universal whole, and that all the universe is God's temple; so that, wheresoever he prays, he shuts his bodily eyes, and, raising the eyes of the soul, he transcends the whole universe.'

79, p. 142. L. Creighton, *Life and Letters of T. Hodgkin*, 1917, p. 240. 'I also feel that if war is absolutely condemned under all circumstances by the Sermon on the Mount, business, as we understand it, is equally condemned....Except on such principle of interpretation as I have suggested, I fear that my forty years of banking life are quite as clearly contrary to the commands of Christ as Lord Roberts's forty years' campaign in India.' The whole of pp. 240–347 should be read in this connection.

80, p. 143. Blake, *Songs of Experience*, 'To Tirzah'; Bossuet, *Dernier Avertissement à M. de Cambray*, quoted in P. Stapfer, *La Grande Prédication en France*, 1898, p. 133.

81, p. 149. I am permitted to say now that this pamphlet was written in collaboration with the late Father Tyrrell. Its two keynotes are to be found in the quotations from Plato and Browning with which it opens and closes.

The extent to which this principle is recognized among other reformers may be illustrated by the following passage. 'Another favourite illustration used by the Bábís (though not, I think, occurring in the Bayan), to explain in what sense the successive manifestations are identical and in what sense progressive, is that of a teacher engaged in teaching different classes of students of different ages and degrees of knowledge. The teacher is the same and his knowledge is the same; but he uses different phraseology and illustrations according to the capacity of his hearers. Thus to a class composed of little children he will perhaps say that knowledge is to be desired because it is sweet like sugar, inasmuch as their minds are incapable of appreciating its desirability in a less concrete and materialistic form; but to a class of older pupils he will describe it in a different manner. So Muhammad, for instance, speaking to a primitive and materialistic people like the Arabs spoke of the resurrection, heaven and hell in terms they could understand; but in the Bayan, which is addressed to a more highly developed and civilized audience, it is explained that...the resurrection of anything is the time when its perfection is made manifest.' Prof. E. G. Browne, *The earliest history of the Bábís*, 1910, Introd. p. xxviii.

**82**, p. 153. Septième édition, 1903, pp. 223 ff.

**83**, p. 156. Cf. the quotation from Canon Newbolt in note 38.

**84**, p. 156. This is true to a certain extent even of Mr C. H. Turner's article in Prof. Swete's volume; but it may be traced far more clearly in the essay of the Dean of Wells. While devoting four pages to a criticism of Harnack's 'charismatic' theory which turns to a great extent on mere verbal differences, the writer entirely ignores a crucial point brought out by Harnack and recently emphasized by the Dean of Carlisle in *The Modern Churchman*, vol. IV. (1914), p. 257. There seems to be clear documentary evidence that 'in Egypt, in the middle of the second century, nothing is known of the alleged necessity of episcopal ordination for a "valid exercise of the ministry."' If Drs Harnack and Rashdall are wrong here, Dr Robinson might profitably have shown where and how they err. If they are right, those three lines of Dr Rashdall's give a more direct answer to Canon Wilson's question than the whole of Dr Robinson's laborious article.

**85**, p. 157. *Essay on the Development of Christian Doctrine*, 1st ed. (1845), p. 240.

**86**, p. 158. In that *locus classicus*, the eleventh chapter of the Epistle to the Hebrews, the first objects of faith are God's existence and his creation of the world; in all the rest of the chapter, the emphasis is on those who are sustained by their faith in that which shall be—on faith not conservative, but adventurous.

**87**, p. 159. Compare Newman's letter of 1872 to Dr Brown, Principal of Aberdeen University (W. Ward, *Life of Cardinal Newman*, 1912, II. 393): 'Never did members of the various Christian communions feel such tenderness for each other, yet never were the obstacles greater or stronger which divide them. What a melancholy thought is this,—and when will a better day come? ...It seems to me that the first step to any chance of unity amid our divisions, is for religious minds, one and all, to live upon the Gospels.' The force of these words is hardly weakened by the fact that Newman's religious position often drove him into utterances of a different tenor.

**88**, p. 159. President Wilson, Dec. 27, 1918.

**89**, p. 159. *Apologeticus*, § 37, slightly abridged.

**90**, p. 160. A. de Vigny, *Moïse*.

# INDEX

# INDEX

CAMBRIDGE: PRINTED BY J. B. PEACE, M.A., AT THE UNIVERSITY PRESS.

*Second Impression*

# SOCIAL LIFE IN BRITAIN
## FROM THE
## CONQUEST TO THE REFORMATION

A Series of Extracts from contemporary writers compiled by

## G. G. COULTON, M.A.

ST CATHARINE'S COLLEGE, CAMBRIDGE

With frontispiece and 4 plates. Demy 8vo. Price 15s net

"It is one of those delightful books that do not demand to be read straight through, but insist, so rich is the store of various information and entertainment, on being read straight on from any page at which the would-be desultory reader may open it. In form it is a collection of extracts from medieval writers, almost all English, 'intended to supply that background of social history which is necessary to a sympathetic comprehension of our own literature of the Middle Ages', and when a man of Mr Coulton's learning and judgment sets himself such a task the result is sure to be a treasury. The fifteen sections cover all the great field from religion to cookery; and, incidentally, they help the general reader to watch the infant growth of our English language and to study the English character under many different lights. The brief introductory notes are models of aptness and selection."
*The Times Literary Supplement*

"To a great many people, I suppose, social history will always make a stronger appeal than political history; and at least it has the advantage over political history that it may be accepted as reliable when we get it in the words of the contemporary historian. But it is not everybody, nowadays, who will read the old chroniclers, the mediaeval monks, or even Froissart himself. I have found a book that will suit them, however —one that skims the cream from all these (which is a dreadful form of book-making, as a rule, but which is most satisfactory in this case), and tells us, by taking a scrap from one man and half a dozen pages from another, what life in England was really like when there were serfs, and feudal lords, and witch-finders, and things of that kind about. It is Mr G. G. Coulton's *Social Life in Britain from the Conquest to the Reformation*, which comes from the Cambridge University Press; and one of its good points is that it may be opened at any page with the certainty that something worth reading, and more or less complete in itself, will be there."—*The Westminster Gazette*

"One of the most charming collections of illustrative passages ever made from old books and documents was Mr Coulton's *Medieval Garner*. Mr Coulton has now compiled the same sort of book about England of the Middle Ages. This is the ideal way to read history— the ideal way, we should say perhaps, to begin to read history. Here we have a world of contemporary evidence as to the food, clothes, religion, sport and morals of the mediaeval Englishman....Mr Coulton's is a most illuminating and instructive book...in which scholars and lovers of literature will delight."—*The Daily News*

CAMBRIDGE UNIVERSITY PRESS
Fetter Lane, London, E.C. 4
C. F. CLAY, Manager

FATHER RHINE. (Barnicott & Pearce, 1899.) 2/6 net

PUBLIC SCHOOLS AND PUBLIC NEEDS. (Barnicott & Pearce, 1900.) 2/- net

FRIAR'S LANTERN. (Barnicott & Pearce, 1906.) 3/6 net

FROM ST FRANCIS TO DANTE. (Duckworth, 1906.) 2nd ed. 12/6 net

CHAUCER AND HIS ENGLAND. (Methuen, 1908.) 2nd ed. 10/6 net

A MEDIEVAL GARNER. (Constable, 1910.) 21/- net

MEDIEVAL STUDIES. First Series. (Simpkin, Marshall & Co. 1914.) 2nd ed. 6/- net

THE MAIN ILLUSIONS OF PACIFICISM. (Bowes & Bowes, 1915.) 5/- net

THE CASE FOR COMPULSORY SERVICE. (Macmillan, 1917.) 7/6 net

SOCIAL LIFE IN BRITAIN FROM THE CON-QUEST TO THE REFORMATION. (Cambridge University Press, 1918.) 2nd impression. 15/- net                    [*See overleaf*